Stone Hill Inn

## STOWE, VERMONT

# The Signature
# Recipe Collection

# The Signature Recipe Collection

Stone Hill Inn, Inc.
Copyright © 2004
Stone Hill Inn, Inc.
89 Houston Farm Road
Stowe, Vermont 05672-4225
802-253-6282
stay@stonehillinn.com

ISBN: 0-9755012-0-8

Edited, Designed, and Manufactured by

**Community**Classics™

An imprint of

FRP

P.O. Box 305142
Nashville, Tennessee 37230
800-358-0560

Manufactured in the United States of America
First Printing: 2004
Number of copies: 5,000

*For all of our loyal guests*
*who make our success possible*

*For reservations, please either call us between*
*8:00 AM and 9:00 PM Eastern, or consult our website at*
*www.stonehillinn.com.*
*On our website, you may see photos of all nine guest rooms,*
*check availability, and make online reservation requests*
*24 hours a day.*

# Table of Contents

# Amy's Acknowledgments

To my Mom and Dad, Linda and Gary Hodgen, I thank you from the bottom
of my heart. I am deeply grateful for your trust and support. As parents,
you taught me so much and did everything you ever could to foster my
independent spirit. Mom, I have to thank you for instilling in me an
appreciation for quality and an eye for detail. When people tell me I have
great taste, I think of you. Additionally, you set the perfect example
as the gracious hostess. Dad, you told me I could accomplish anything
I set out to do if I really tried. Thank you for that lesson.
Your professional career has been a grand example. Throughout this endeavor,
your keen business sense, entrepreneurial spirit, and courage to
"break the mold" have been an inspiration to both me and Hap.
To Michele, my sister, thank you for teaching me so much about the seasonality
of foods, the importance of using the best ingredients, and the pairing
of good flavors and textures. You gave me the opportunity to try my hand
at the restaurant business as your partner. That experience lent me so much
knowledge prior to opening the Inn. And, of course, without that chapter
of my life and you, I never would have met my husband!

# Hap's Acknowledgments

*I would like to thank both my grandmothers, Stella Jordan and Ima Asbell,*
*and, of course, my mother, Jackie Dessoffy. I would like to express*
*my appreciation for their believing in me and giving me direction when needed.*
*Each of you did your part to instill a strong work ethic in me.*
*Love to all of you!*

*We both wish to thank Rob Roper for his assistance*
*in writing our cookbook's introduction and back cover copy.*
*We must credit Glenn Moody for the wonderful photos*
*on the front and back covers. Sally Stetson created the leaf images*
*that adorn all the pages. We also would like to thank FRP for their guidance*
*in making this cookbook possible.*

## Introduction

"Made from scratch." The words should be carved into the rocks on which the Stone Hill Inn was built. This ultimate romantic hideaway is the dream child, from the ground up, of owners Amy and Hap Jordan. Their wonderful vision of a sanctuary— one in which every element that romance needs to thrive is provided in its most luxurious incarnation—is now their customers' blissful reality.

From fireside Jacuzzis in every room, to the finest linens on every king-size bed, to magical garden walks where a hammock or bench is waiting for you in just the right spot, every detail is carefully crafted, charmingly executed. And the thread that weaves its way delightfully through the passage of each day is good, good food.

Open the door of the Stone Hill Inn and the first thing that strikes you is the welcoming aroma of evening hors d'ouevre. Returning guests know to bring along a bottle of their favorite wine, as well as the best places to cozy up with a plate to share—by the fire, in the gardens, or just back in their rooms. The next morning, guests pleasantly wake to the enticing smells of breakfast drifting from the kitchen. The morning meal is a grand experience worth getting out of even a supremely comfortable bed to enjoy. Tables are set for two in a window-walled breakfast room with candlelight and soft music.

Indeed, the food, generously served and artfully presented, is one of the highlights of the Stone Hill Inn experience. So, it's no wonder that so many guests of the Stone Hill Inn leave, arm in arm, with the hopeful advice, "You ought to write a cookbook." And now, Amy and Hap, accustomed to making their guests' dreams come true, have done just that. This cookbook is a collection of favorite recipes that have been tested time and time again by the innkeepers and repeatedly requested by the guests who have enjoyed them. They hope that you'll find these recipes useful for family breakfasts, romantic breakfasts in bed, holiday celebrations, elegant entertaining, backyard get-togethers with close friends, and intimate, light fireside suppers for two.

Neither Amy nor Hap Jordan is a professionally trained chef. They learned to cook the same way they learned to run one of North America's most highly regarded inns— with a vision, with creativity, with attention to detail, and, of course, with a loving desire to make something wonderful "from scratch."

# Fresh Fruit Dishes

## Grand Fruit Salad

2 cups green seedless grapes
2 cups sliced strawberries
2 cups sliced peeled plums
1 cup sliced peeled peaches
1 cup orange sections, cut into 1-inch pieces
1 cup sliced kiwifruit
1½ cups orange liqueur
½ cup orange juice
2 tablespoons sugar

Combine the grapes, strawberries, plums, peaches, oranges and kiwifruit in a large bowl. Stir the orange liqueur, orange juice and sugar in a bowl until well mixed. Pour over the fruit and toss gently to coat. Cover and chill until ready to serve.

Yield: 8 servings

# Fruit Salad with Honey-Lime Dressing

1/2 cup plain yogurt
1/4 cup honey
1 teaspoon grated lime zest
1/4 cup fresh lime juice
2 cups cantaloupe chunks
2 cups honeydew melon chunks
2 cups red seedless grapes
2 cups fresh pineapple chunks
1 1/2 cups fresh papaya chunks
1 cup halved strawberries

Mix the yogurt, honey, lime zest and lime juice in a small bowl.
Cover and chill. Combine the cantaloupe, honeydew melon, grapes,
pineapple, papaya and strawberries in a large bowl. Cover and chill.
Add the dressing to the fruit 15 minutes before serving and toss
gently to coat. Let stand at room temperature for 15 minutes to allow
flavors to blend.

Yield: 8 servings

# Fruit Salad with Honey and Rum

3 tablespoons honey
3 tablespoons dark rum
1 large orange, peeled and cut into 1-inch sections
1 large Fuji or Golden Delicious apple, unpeeled,
cored and cut into chunks
1 pear, unpeeled, cored and cut into chunks
1 banana, sliced
1 cup green seedless grapes
1 cup strawberry halves
1/2 cup raspberries
1/2 cup blueberries

Whisk the honey and rum in a large bowl. Add the orange sections, apple chunks, pear chunks, banana slices, grapes, strawberries, raspberries and blueberries. Stir gently to mix well. Cover and chill for at least 30 minutes and up to 4 hours before serving.

Yield: 6 servings

## Wake Up Fruit Plate

1 honeydew melon, seeded and cut into slices
1/2 cup vanilla yogurt
4 ounces cream cheese, softened
2 tablespoons honey
1/2 cup fresh raspberries

Divide the honeydew melon slices among 4 plates. Process the yogurt, cream cheese and honey in a blender. Pour over the honeydew melon slices and sprinkle with the raspberries.

Yield: 4 servings

## Mixed Fruit Bowl

3 cups strawberries, sliced
2 tablespoons sugar
2 oranges, peeled and cut into 1-inch sections
1 kiwifruit, sliced
1 banana, sliced
1 cup blueberries
1 cup red seedless grapes

Combine the strawberries and sugar in a large bowl. Stir gently to mix. Add the oranges, kiwifruit, banana, blueberries and grapes. Stir gently to mix well and serve.

Yield: 6 servings

# Honey, Mint and Lime Fruit Bowl

1/4 cup fresh lime juice
1/4 cup honey
1/4 cup chopped fresh mint
1 cantaloupe, halved and seeded
1 (12-ounce) container fresh strawberries, hulled and halved
4 kiwifruit, sliced
1 1/2 cups red or green seedless grapes

Whisk the lime juice, honey and mint in a large bowl. Scoop out the cantaloupe with a melon baller. Add the melon balls, strawberries, kiwifruit and grapes to the lime juice mixture. Toss gently to mix. Let stand for 15 minutes before serving or cover and chill for up to 3 hours.

Yield: 8 servings

# Honeydew in Lemon Thyme Syrup

1 cup water
1/2 cup sugar
1/4 cup chopped fresh lemon thyme
1 1/2 honeydew melons, seeded and
cut into bite-size pieces or balls

Combine the water, sugar and lemon thyme in a 1-quart saucepan. Bring to a boil over medium-high heat, stirring until the sugar dissolves. Boil for 5 to 10 minutes or until reduced to 3/4 cup. Remove from the heat and let stand at room temperature for 30 minutes. Strain through a sieve into a bowl, pressing on the lemon thyme to release its flavor. Discard the lemon thyme. Arrange the melon pieces in a shallow serving bowl. Drizzle with the syrup and serve within 1 hour.

Yield: 8 servings

*Note:* You may substitute regular fresh thyme and the juice of 1/2 lemon if lemon thyme is unavailable.

## Melon Ball Mix

2 cantaloupe, halved and seeded
1 honeydew melon, halved and seeded
1 cup orange juice
1/2 cup honey
1 teaspoon cinnamon

Scoop out the cantaloupe and honeydew melon with a melon baller into a large bowl. Stir the orange juice, honey and cinnamon in a bowl until blended. Add to the melon balls. Mix well and serve.

Yield: 12 servings

## Coconut Fruit Bowl

1 (11-ounce) can mandarin oranges, drained
2 bananas, sliced
1/2 fresh pineapple, cut into chunks
1/2 cup flaked coconut

Combine the oranges, bananas, pineapple and coconut in a bowl. Toss gently to mix and serve.

Yield: 6 servings

# Fruit and Champagne Compotes

3 small grapefruits, peeled
1 cup raspberries
1 teaspoon sugar
2 kiwifruit, sliced
1 cup chilled Champagne
4 fresh mint sprigs for garnish

Section the grapefruits over a large bowl to catch any juice. Add the grapefruit sections to the bowl. Add the raspberries and sprinkle with the sugar. Stir gently to mix. Cover and chill. Stir in the kiwifruit gently just before serving. Add the Champagne slowly and mix gently. Spoon the mixture into 4 footed compote dishes and top each with a sprig of mint.

Yield: 4 servings

# Muffins, Breads, Scones & Coffee Cakes

# Morning Glory Muffins

2¼ cups flour
1¼ cups sugar
1 tablespoon cinnamon
2 teaspoons baking soda
½ teaspoon salt
3 eggs
¾ cup applesauce
½ cup canola oil
1 teaspoon vanilla extract
2 cups grated carrots
1 Granny Smith apple, peeled, cored and grated
1 (8-ounce) can crushed pineapple, drained
½ cup flaked coconut
½ cup raisins
½ cup chopped walnuts

Mix the flour, sugar, cinnamon, baking soda and salt in a large bowl. Beat the eggs, applesauce, oil and vanilla in a bowl. Add to the dry ingredients and stir until just moistened; the batter will be thick. Stir in the carrots, apple, pineapple, coconut, raisins and walnuts. Fill greased muffin cups ⅔ full. Bake at 350 degrees for 22 to 24 minutes or until the tops spring back when touched. Cool in the pans for 5 minutes. Remove to a wire rack to cool completely.

Yield: 24 muffins

*Note:* These are so moist and delicious.

## Apple Walnut Muffins

2 eggs, lightly beaten
1/2 cup canola oil
2 teaspoons vanilla extract
4 cups chopped peeled apples
1 cup sugar
2 cups flour
2 teaspoons baking soda
1 teaspoon cinnamon
1 teaspoon salt
1 cup raisins
1 cup walnut pieces

Beat the eggs, oil and vanilla in a large bowl. Mix the apples and sugar in a bowl. Stir into the egg mixture. Combine the flour, baking soda, cinnamon and salt in a bowl. Add to the apple mixture and stir until just combined. Fold in the raisins and walnuts. Fill greased muffin cups 2/3 full. Bake at 325 degrees for 30 minutes or until a wooden pick inserted in the center comes out clean. Cool in the pans for 5 minutes. Remove to a wire rack to cool completely.

Yield: 24 muffins

## Old-Fashioned Applesauce Muffins

2 cups flour
1 cup sugar
2 teaspoons baking soda
1 teaspoon cinnamon
$\frac{1}{2}$ teaspoon nutmeg
$\frac{1}{8}$ teaspoon allspice
$\frac{1}{8}$ teaspoon salt
$1\frac{1}{2}$ cups unsweetened applesauce
$\frac{1}{2}$ cup (1 stick) butter, melted
$\frac{1}{2}$ cup raisins

Mix the flour, sugar, baking soda, cinnamon, nutmeg, allspice and salt in a large bowl. Whisk the applesauce and melted butter in a bowl. Add to the dry ingredients and stir until just moistened. Add the raisins and stir gently to mix. Fill greased muffin cups $\frac{2}{3}$ full. Bake at 375 degrees for 20 minutes or until golden brown and a wooden pick inserted in the center comes out clean. Cool in the pans for 10 minutes. Remove to a wire rack to cool completely.

Yield: 15 muffins

# Banana Walnut Muffins

½ cup canola oil
1 cup sugar
2 eggs, beaten
3 bananas, chopped
2 cups flour
1 teaspoon baking soda
½ teaspoon baking powder
½ teaspoon salt
3 tablespoons buttermilk
1 teaspoon vanilla extract
½ cup chopped walnuts

Beat the oil and sugar in a large bowl. Add the eggs and bananas and beat well. Stir the flour, baking soda, baking powder and salt in a bowl. Add to the banana mixture along with the buttermilk and vanilla. Beat well to mix. Stir in the walnuts. Fill greased muffin cups ⅔ full. Bake at 350 degrees for 26 minutes or until a wooden pick inserted in the center comes out clean. Cool in the pans for 5 minutes. Remove to a wire rack to cool completely.

Yield: 15 muffins

## *Easy Banana Muffins*

3 large ripe bananas
3/4 cup sugar
1 egg, lightly beaten
5 1/3 tablespoons unsalted butter, melted
1 1/2 cups flour
1 teaspoon baking powder
1 teaspoon baking soda
1/2 teaspoon salt

Mash the bananas in a large bowl. Add the sugar and egg and mix well. Stir in the melted butter. Combine the flour, baking powder, baking soda and salt in a bowl. Add to the banana mixture and stir to mix. Fill greased muffin cups 2/3 full. Bake at 375 degrees for 20 minutes or until firm to the touch. Cool in the pan for 5 minutes. Remove to a wire rack to cool completely.

Yield: 12 muffins

# Blueberry Sour Cream Muffins

2 eggs
1 cup sugar
1/2 cup vegetable oil
1/2 teaspoon vanilla extract
2 cups flour
1 teaspoon baking powder
1/2 teaspoon baking soda
1/2 teaspoon salt
1 cup sour cream
1 cup fresh blueberries

Beat the eggs in a bowl. Beat in the sugar gradually. Beat in the oil gradually and stir in the vanilla. Mix the flour, baking powder, baking soda and salt in a large bowl. Stir in the sour cream alternately with the egg mixture. Fold in the blueberries. Fill well-greased muffin cups 2/3 full. Bake at 400 degrees for 20 to 25 minutes or until a wooden pick inserted in the center comes out clean. Cool in the pans for 5 minutes. Remove to a wire rack to cool completely.

Yield: 16 muffins

## Cranberry Orange Muffins

2$\frac{1}{2}$ cups all-purpose flour
1 cup whole wheat flour
1$\frac{1}{2}$ cups sugar
2 tablespoons baking powder
$\frac{1}{2}$ teaspoon salt
4$\frac{1}{2}$ teaspoons grated orange zest
4 egg whites
1$\frac{1}{4}$ cups orange juice
$\frac{1}{4}$ cup orange liqueur
$\frac{3}{4}$ cup canola oil
2 cups chopped cranberries

Mix the all-purpose flour, whole wheat flour, sugar, baking powder, salt and orange zest in a large bowl. Beat the egg whites in a bowl until frothy. Stir in the orange juice, orange liqueur and oil. Add to the dry ingredients along with the cranberries. Stir until just moistened. Fill paper-lined muffin cups $\frac{3}{4}$ full. Bake at 400 degrees for 25 minutes or until golden brown and puffed. Cool in the pans for 5 minutes. Remove to a wire rack to cool completely.

Yield: 24 muffins

## Lemon Muffins

2 cups flour
1 teaspoon baking powder
1 teaspoon baking soda
1/4 teaspoon salt
1/4 cup sugar
2 tablespoons honey
2 eggs
1 1/4 cups plain yogurt, at room temperature
1/4 cup (1/2 stick) butter, melted
1 tablespoon grated lemon zest
1/3 cup sugar
1/3 cup fresh lemon juice
3 tablespoons water

Combine the flour, baking powder, baking soda and salt in a bowl. Mix 1/4 cup sugar, the honey, eggs, yogurt, melted butter and lemon zest in a large bowl. Add the dry ingredients and stir until just combined. Fill greased muffin cups 2/3 full. Bake at 375 degrees for 15 minutes or until a wooden pick inserted in the center comes out clean. Cool in the pan for 5 minutes. Remove to a plate. Combine 1/3 cup sugar, the lemon juice and water in a small saucepan. Bring to a boil and boil for 1 minute. Drizzle over the warm muffins.

Yield: 12 muffins

## Orange Yogurt Muffins

3 large oranges
1/4 cup sugar
2 tablespoons water
5 tablespoons unsalted butter
2 cups flour
1/4 cup sugar
1 1/4 teaspoons baking powder
1 teaspoon baking soda
1/2 teaspoon salt
2 eggs
3/4 cup plain yogurt
3/4 cup milk
1 cup confectioners' sugar
2 tablespoons fresh orange juice
Pinch of salt

Grate the zest from the oranges into a saucepan. Remove 2 teaspoons to a small bowl and reserve. Add 1/4 cup sugar and the water to the saucepan. Cook over medium heat for 2 minutes, stirring until the sugar dissolves. Add the butter and cook until the butter melts, stirring constantly. Remove from the heat and let cool. Combine the flour, 1/4 cup sugar, baking powder, baking soda and 1/2 teaspoon salt in a bowl. Whisk the eggs, yogurt, milk and cooled orange zest mixture in a large bowl. Add the dry ingredients and stir until just combined. Fill greased muffin cups 3/4 full. Bake at 375 degrees for 16 minutes or until just starting to brown. Cool in the pans for 3 minutes. Remove to a plate. Add the confectioners' sugar, orange juice and pinch of salt to the reserved orange zest. Stir to mix well. Thin with additional orange juice, if necessary. Drizzle over the warm muffins.

Yield: 14 muffins

## Ginger Peach Muffins

2 cups flour
2 teaspoons baking powder
1 teaspoon ginger
1/2 teaspoon salt
1/2 teaspoon cinnamon
1/4 teaspoon ground cloves
1/2 cup sugar
1/2 cup unsweetened applesauce
1/4 cup apple juice
1/4 cup molasses
1 egg
2 tablespoons canola oil
1 1/2 cups chopped peeled fresh peaches

Mix the flour, baking powder, ginger, salt, cinnamon and cloves in a large bowl. Whisk the sugar, applesauce, apple juice, molasses, egg, oil and peaches in a bowl. Add to the dry ingredients and stir until just moistened. Fill greased muffin cups 2/3 full. Bake at 400 degrees for 20 minutes or until a wooden pick inserted in the center comes out clean. Cool in the pan for 15 minutes. Remove to a wire rack to cool completely.

Yield: 12 muffins

# Pumpkin Muffins

2 cups sugar
1/2 cup canola oil
3 eggs
1 1/2 cups canned pumpkin
1/2 cup water
3 cups flour
1 1/2 teaspoons baking powder
1 teaspoon baking soda
1 teaspoon salt
3/4 teaspoon cinnamon
1/2 teaspoon cloves
1/2 teaspoon nutmeg
1 1/2 cups raisins
1 cup chopped walnuts

Whisk the sugar, oil, eggs, pumpkin and water in a large bowl. Mix the flour, baking powder, baking soda, salt, cinnamon, cloves, and nutmeg in a bowl. Add to the pumpkin mixture and stir until just combined. Stir in the raisins and walnuts gently. Let stand for 1 hour at room temperature. Fill greased muffin cups 2/3 full. Bake at 400 degrees for 15 minutes or until a wooden pick inserted in the center comes out clean. Cool in the pans for 5 minutes. Remove to a wire rack to cool completely.

Yield: 24 muffins

# Strawberry Orange Muffins

2¼ cups flour
2 teaspoons baking powder
1 teaspoon baking soda
½ teaspoon salt
¾ cup sugar
½ cup milk
½ cup sour cream
⅓ cup canola oil
1 egg
1 tablespoon grated orange zest
1 cup thinly sliced fresh strawberries, drained on paper towels
⅓ cup strawberry jam

Mix the flour, baking powder, baking soda and salt in a large bowl.
Whisk the sugar, milk, sour cream, oil, egg and orange zest in a
bowl. Stir in the strawberries. Add to the dry ingredients and stir
until just combined. Place a spoonful of batter in each greased
muffin cup. Top each with a scant teaspoonful of strawberry jam.
Fill each muffin cup ⅔ full with the remaining batter. Bake at
400 degrees for 15 to 18 minutes or until a wooden pick inserted
in the center comes out clean. Cool in the pans for 5 minutes.
Remove to a wire rack to cool completely.

Yield: 16 muffins

# Chocolate Cheesecake Muffins

8 ounces cream cheese, softened
2 tablespoons sugar
1 cup flour
1/2 cup sugar
3 tablespoons baking cocoa
2 teaspoons baking powder
1/2 teaspoon salt
1/2 cup milk chocolate chips
1 egg, beaten
3/4 cup milk
1/3 cup canola oil
Confectioners' sugar

Beat the cream cheese and 2 tablespoons sugar in a bowl with an electric mixer until fluffy; set aside. Mix the flour, 1/2 cup sugar, baking cocoa, baking powder, salt and chocolate chips in a large bowl. Whisk the egg, milk and oil in a small bowl. Add to the dry ingredients and stir until just moistened; the batter will be lumpy. Place a spoonful of batter in each paper-lined muffin cup. Top with a teaspoonful of the cream cheese mixture in the center of each cup. Fill each muffin cup 2/3 full with the remaining batter to cover the cream cheese mixture. Bake at 375 degrees for 20 minutes or until the tops spring back when touched. Cool in the pan for 20 minutes. Remove to a wire rack to cool completely. Dust with confectioners' sugar before serving.

Yield: 12 muffins

*Note:* Serve a couple of these with a bowl of fresh strawberries for a romantic breakfast in bed.

## Miniature Mocha Macadamia Muffins

1¼ cups flour
⅔ cup sugar
2 to 3 tablespoons baking cocoa
1 teaspoon baking soda
¼ teaspoon salt
1 tablespoon instant coffee powder
1 tablespoon hot water
⅔ cup buttermilk
3 tablespoons unsalted butter, melted
1 egg, beaten
¾ teaspoon coffee liqueur
½ cup chopped macadamia nuts
Confectioners' sugar

Mix the flour, sugar, baking cocoa, baking soda and salt in a large
bowl. Dissolve the coffee powder in the hot water in a cup.
Whisk the buttermilk, melted butter, egg, dissolved coffee and
coffee liqueur in a bowl. Add to the dry ingredients and stir until
just moistened. Fold in the macadamia nuts. Fill greased miniature
muffin cups ⅔ full. Bake at 400 degrees for 14 minutes or until
firm to the touch. Cool in the pans for 5 minutes. Remove to a wire
rack to cool completely. Dust with confectioners' sugar before serving.

Yield: 24 muffins

*Note:* This recipe originally comes from the Evergreen Inn
in Spring Lake, New Jersey.

# Miniature Cinnamon Spice Muffins

1¹/₂ cups flour
¹/₂ cup sugar
2 teaspoons baking powder
¹/₂ teaspoon salt
¹/₂ teaspoon nutmeg
¹/₂ teaspoon allspice
1 egg, lightly beaten
¹/₂ cup fat-free milk
5¹/₃ tablespoons unsalted butter, melted
2 tablespoons sugar
¹/₂ teaspoon cinnamon
¹/₄ cup (¹/₂ stick) unsalted butter, melted

Mix the flour, ¹/₂ cup sugar, baking powder, salt, nutmeg and allspice in a large bowl. Whisk the egg, milk and 5¹/₃ tablespoons melted butter in a bowl. Add to the dry ingredients and stir until just moistened. Fill greased miniature muffin cups ³/₄ full. Bake at 400 degrees for 13 minutes or until a wooden pick inserted in the center comes out clean. Cool in the pans for 3 to 4 minutes. Mix 2 tablespoons sugar and the cinnamon in a small bowl. Brush the tops of the hot muffins with ¹/₄ cup melted butter. Sprinkle with the cinnamon-sugar. Remove the muffins to a wire rack to cool.

Yield: 24 muffins

# Cinnamon Crunch Muffins

3 cups flour
1 1/2 cups packed brown sugar
1/2 teaspoon salt
1 teaspoon cinnamon
1 teaspoon ginger
2/3 cup shortening
1/2 cup chopped walnuts or pecans
1 teaspoon cinnamon
2 teaspoons baking powder
1/2 teaspoon baking soda
2 eggs, beaten
1 cup buttermilk

Mix the flour, brown sugar, salt, 1 teaspoon cinnamon and ginger in a large bowl. Add the shortening and mix with fingertips until crumbly. Remove 2/3 cup of the mixture to a small bowl. Add the walnuts and 1 teaspoon cinnamon to the small bowl. Stir to mix and set aside for topping. Add the baking powder and baking soda to the shortening mixture in the large bowl and stir until just blended. Add the eggs and buttermilk and stir until just combined. Fill greased muffin cups 2/3 full. Sprinkle the reserved topping evenly over the muffins. Bake at 375 degrees for 17 to 22 minutes or until a wooden pick inserted in the center comes out clean. Cool in the pans for 3 to 5 minutes. Remove to a wire rack to cool completely.

Yield: 16 muffins

# Honey-Glazed Gingerbread Muffins

### MUFFINS
1 3/4 cups flour
1/3 cup packed brown sugar
1/4 cup sugar
1 tablespoon baking powder
1 teaspoon cinnamon
1 teaspoon ginger
1/2 teaspoon nutmeg
1/2 teaspoon baking soda
1 cup buttermilk
1/2 cup (1 stick) unsalted butter, melted
1/4 cup molasses
2 eggs

### TOPPING
1/3 cup packed brown sugar
1/3 cup sugar
1/4 cup (1/2 stick) unsalted butter, softened
3 tablespoons honey, at room temperature
1 tablespoon water

*For the muffins,* mix the flour, brown sugar, sugar, baking powder, cinnamon, ginger, nutmeg and baking soda in a large bowl. Whisk the buttermilk, melted butter, molasses and eggs in a bowl. Add to the dry ingredients and stir until just moistened. Fill greased muffin cups 3/4 full. Bake at 400 degrees for 15 minutes or until firm to the touch. Cool in the pans for 10 minutes. Remove to a serving platter.

*For the topping,* beat the brown sugar, sugar and softened butter in a bowl until fluffy. Beat in the honey and water. Spread evenly on top of the warm muffins.

Yield: 18 muffins

# Maple Walnut Muffins

1¼ cups flour
1 cup rolled oats
1 cup chopped walnuts
½ cup packed brown sugar
1 teaspoon baking powder
½ teaspoon baking soda
½ teaspoon salt
1 cup sour cream
5 tablespoons butter, softened
2 eggs
½ cup real Vermont maple syrup
(Dark Amber or Grade B)

Mix the flour, oats, walnuts, brown sugar, baking powder, baking soda and salt in a large bowl. Beat the sour cream, butter, eggs and maple syrup in a bowl until smooth. Add to the dry ingredients and stir until just moistened. Fill well-greased muffin cups ⅔ full. Bake at 350 degrees for 25 minutes or until a wooden pick inserted in the center comes out clean. Cool in the pan for 10 minutes. Remove to a wire rack to cool completely.

Yield: 12 muffins

## Orange Toasted Almond Muffins

2½ cups flour
1 cup sugar
3½ teaspoons baking powder
½ teaspoon salt
¼ teaspoon almond extract
1 tablespoon grated orange zest
⅓ cup canola oil
¾ cup evaporated milk
½ cup water
1 egg
¾ cup finely chopped toasted almonds
1 cup confectioners' sugar
4½ teaspoons orange juice
¼ cup finely chopped toasted almonds

Combine the flour, sugar, baking powder, salt, almond extract, orange zest, oil, evaporated milk, water and egg in a large bowl. Beat with an electric mixer at high speed for 30 seconds. Fold in ¾ cup almonds. Fill greased muffin cups ⅔ full. Bake at 375 degrees for 15 to 18 minutes or until a wooden pick inserted in the center comes out clean. Cool in the pans for 5 minutes. Remove to a wire rack to cool completely. Stir the confectioners' sugar and orange juice in a small bowl until smooth. Spread evenly on top of the muffins and sprinkle with ¼ cup almonds.

Yield: 18 muffins

# Oat and Jam Muffins

1 cup rolled oats
1 cup buttermilk
1 egg, beaten
1/2 cup (1 stick) unsalted butter, melted
1 cup flour
1/2 cup packed brown sugar
2 teaspoons baking powder
1 teaspoon baking soda
1/2 teaspoon salt
3/4 cup strawberry, raspberry or peach jam

Stir the oats and buttermilk in a large bowl until the oats are
moistened. Add the egg and melted butter and stir to mix well.
Mix the flour, brown sugar, baking powder, baking soda and salt
in a bowl. Add to the oat mixture and stir until just combined. Fill
greased muffin cups 2/3 full. Spoon a scant teaspoonful of jam on
top of each muffin; do not make a hole in the batter. Bake at
350 degrees for 15 minutes or until firm to the touch. Cool in the
pans for 5 minutes. Remove to a wire rack to cool completely.

Yield: 15 muffins

# Apple Raisin Bread

3 cups flour
2 1/2 cups sugar
2 teaspoons cinnamon
1 teaspoon ground cloves
1 1/2 teaspoons baking soda
1/2 teaspoon baking powder
4 eggs, beaten
1 1/4 cups canola oil
1 tablespoon vanilla extract
3 cups chopped unpeeled apples
1/2 cup raisins
1/2 cup chopped walnuts (optional)

Mix the flour, sugar, cinnamon, cloves, baking soda and baking powder in a large bowl. Add the eggs, oil, vanilla, apples, raisins and walnuts and stir to mix well. Pour the batter into 2 greased 5×9-inch loaf pans and smooth the tops. Bake at 325 degrees for 1 hour and 30 minutes or until a wooden pick inserted in the center comes out clean. Cool in the pans for 1 hour. Remove to a wire rack to cool completely.

Yield: 2 loaves

*Note:* This bread must be fully baked, or it will be soggy in the center.

# Banana Bread with Coconut and Macadamia Nuts

2¼ cups flour
¾ teaspoon baking powder
½ teaspoon baking soda
1 teaspoon salt
¾ cup (1½ sticks) unsalted butter, softened
1 cup packed brown sugar
½ cup sugar
3 eggs
1½ teaspoons vanilla extract
1 tablespoon grated lemon zest
1⅓ cups mashed ripe bananas (about 3 large bananas)
3 tablespoons sour cream
¾ cup chopped macadamia nuts
1 cup flaked coconut, lightly toasted and cooled

Sift the flour, baking powder, baking soda and salt into a bowl. Beat the butter, brown sugar and sugar in a large bowl with an electric mixer at medium speed until light and fluffy. Beat in the eggs 1 at a time. Add the vanilla, lemon zest, mashed bananas and sour cream. Beat until well mixed. Add the dry ingredients and beat until just combined. Stir in the macadamia nuts and coconut. Spoon the batter into 5 greased and floured 3¼×5¾-inch loaf pans and smooth the tops. Bake at 350 degrees for 35 to 40 minutes or until a wooden pick inserted in the center comes out clean. Cool in the pans for 10 minutes. Remove to a wire rack to cool completely.

Yield: 5 loaves

*Note:* This bread freezes well and also is a nice size for gift-giving.

# Banana Chocolate Chip Nut Bread

1½ cups sugar
½ cup (1 stick) butter, softened
2 eggs
2¼ cups flour
¾ teaspoon baking soda
½ teaspoon baking powder
½ teaspoon salt
1¼ cups mashed ripe bananas (about 3 bananas)
1 teaspoon vanilla extract
¼ cup buttermilk
1 cup chopped walnuts
1 cup semisweet chocolate chips

Beat the sugar and butter in a large bowl with an electric mixer at medium speed until light and fluffy. Beat in the eggs 1 at a time. Mix the flour, baking soda, baking powder and salt in a bowl. Add to the butter mixture and beat well. Mix the mashed bananas, vanilla, buttermilk, walnuts and chocolate chips in a bowl. Add to the flour mixture and beat well. Pour the batter into a large loaf pan coated with nonstick cooking spray and smooth the top. Bake at 350 degrees for 1 hour and 15 minutes or until a wooden pick inserted in the center comes out clean. Cool in the pan for 10 minutes. Remove to a wire rack to cool completely.

Yield: 1 loaf

*Note:* In order for the center of the bread to be fully baked, the corners will be overdone. Remove and discard the outside slices, if desired. This is an extremely popular recipe with our guests.

# Cranberry Orange Nut Bread

2 cups flour
3/4 cup sugar
1 1/2 teaspoons baking powder
1 teaspoon salt
1/2 teaspoon baking soda
3/4 cup orange juice
1 egg, beaten
2 tablespoons canola oil
1 cup chopped fresh or frozen cranberries
1/2 cup chopped walnuts

Mix the flour, sugar, baking powder, salt and baking soda in a large bowl. Mix the orange juice, egg and oil in a bowl. Add to the dry ingredients and stir until just moistened. Fold in the cranberries and walnuts. Spoon the batter into a greased and floured 5×9-inch or 4 1/2×12-inch loaf pan. Bake at 350 degrees for 50 to 60 minutes or until a wooden pick inserted in the center comes out clean. Cool in the pan for 20 minutes. Remove to a wire rack to cool completely.

Yield: 1 loaf

# Ginger Pear Bread

1½ cups flour
¾ cup sugar
1 teaspoon baking powder
1 teaspoon baking soda
1 teaspoon ginger
½ teaspoon salt
2 ripe pears, peeled, cored and coarsely chopped
⅔ cup milk
⅓ cup canola oil
1 egg
1 teaspoon vanilla extract

Mix the flour, sugar, baking powder, baking soda, ginger and salt in a large bowl. Add the pears and toss to coat. Mix the milk, oil, egg and vanilla in a bowl. Add to the pear mixture and stir gently until just moistened; the batter will be lumpy. Pour the batter into a greased and floured 5×9-inch or 4½×12-inch loaf pan. Bake at 350 degrees for 60 to 65 minutes or until a wooden pick inserted in the center comes out clean. Cool in the pan for 30 minutes. Remove to a wire rack to cool completely.

Yield: 1 loaf

## Pineapple Zucchini Bread

3 eggs, lightly beaten
1 cup canola oil
2 cups sugar
2 cups grated zucchini
1 tablespoon vanilla extract
3 cups flour
1 tablespoon cinnamon
1 teaspoon baking soda
1 teaspoon salt
1 cup chopped walnuts
1 (8-ounce) can crushed pineapple
Softened cream cheese

Mix the eggs, oil, sugar, zucchini and vanilla in a large bowl. Mix the flour, cinnamon, baking soda and salt in a bowl. Add to the zucchini mixture and stir to mix. Add the walnuts and pineapple and stir to mix. Spread the batter into 2 greased loaf pans. Bake at 350 degrees for 50 minutes or until a wooden pick inserted in the center comes out clean. Cool in the pans for 45 minutes. Remove to a wire rack to cool completely. Slice and serve with softened cream cheese.

Yield: 2 loaves

*Note:* If using large, mature zucchini, remove the seeds before grating by hand or in a food processor.

# Pumpkin Bread

3½ cups flour
3 cups sugar
2 teaspoons baking soda
1½ teaspoons salt
2 teaspoons cinnamon
2 teaspoons allspice
1 teaspoon nutmeg
1 cup canola oil
1 (16-ounce) can pumpkin
⅔ cup water
4 eggs, beaten
1 cup raisins

Mix the flour, sugar, baking soda, salt, cinnamon, allspice and nutmeg in a large bowl. Add the oil, pumpkin, water, eggs and raisins and stir to mix well. Spread the batter into 2 greased 5×9-inch loaf pans. Bake at 350 degrees for 1 hour or until a wooden pick inserted in the center comes out clean. Cool in the pans for 10 minutes. Remove to a wire rack to cool completely.

Yield: 2 loaves

*Note:* This moist and flavorful bread is a big hit during our beautiful fall foliage season.

## Cherry Almond Scones

2¾ cups flour
⅓ cup sugar
¼ cup buttermilk powder or dry milk powder
1 tablespoon baking powder
¾ teaspoon salt
½ cup (1 stick) chilled unsalted butter, cut into pieces
¾ cup dried cherries
2 eggs
¾ teaspoon almond extract
¾ cup milk
Sugar

Mix the flour, ⅓ cup sugar, buttermilk powder, baking powder and salt in a large bowl. Cut in the butter with a pastry blender until crumbly. Add the cherries and toss to coat. Whisk the eggs, almond extract and milk in a bowl. Add to the dry ingredients and stir until the dough just holds together; the dough will be stiff. Thin with a little milk if too stiff. Knead the dough on a lightly floured surface 3 or 4 times. Shape into a disk. Cut into 8 wedges using a large knife. Place ½ inch apart on a lightly greased baking sheet and sprinkle with additional sugar. Bake at 425 degrees for 15 to 18 minutes or until firm in the center and golden brown on top. Cool on the baking sheet for 10 minutes. Remove the scones to a wire rack to cool completely.

Yield: 8 servings

## Oatmeal Currant Scones

1¾ cups flour
⅓ cup sugar
1½ teaspoons baking powder
¾ teaspoon baking soda
½ teaspoon salt
¾ cup (1½ sticks) chilled unsalted butter,
cut into pieces
1⅓ cups rolled oats
½ cup dried currants
½ cup buttermilk
1 egg, lightly beaten
Cinnamon-sugar

Mix the flour, sugar, baking powder, baking soda and salt in a large bowl. Cut in the butter with a pastry blender until crumbly. Stir in the oats and currants. Add the buttermilk and stir first with a wooden spoon and then mix with hands until it just forms a sticky dough. Form into a ball and knead on a lightly floured surface 4 or 5 times. Roll out to a ¾-inch-thick circle with a floured rolling pin. Cut out rounds with a 3-inch biscuit cutter. Gather the dough scraps and roll them out. Cut out more rounds. Place the scones on a lightly greased baking sheet. Brush the tops with the beaten egg and sprinkle with cinnamon-sugar. Bake at 375 degrees for 18 to 20 minutes or until light golden brown. Remove the scones to a wire rack to cool completely.

Yield: 8 to 10 scones

## Piña Colada Scones

2½ cups flour
¼ cup measures-like-sugar granular artificial sweetener
2 teaspoons baking powder
¾ teaspoon baking soda
½ teaspoon salt
¼ teaspoon cinnamon
1 cup light piña colada yogurt
¼ cup egg substitute
¼ cup undrained juice-pack crushed pineapple
1 teaspoon coconut extract
Sugar (optional)

Mix the flour, artificial sweetener, baking powder, baking soda, salt and cinnamon in a large bowl. Mix the yogurt, egg substitute, pineapple and coconut extract in a bowl. Add to the dry ingredients and stir until just moistened. Knead the dough on a lightly floured surface 3 or 4 times. Divide the dough in half and shape each half into a disk. Cut each into 6 wedges using a large knife. Place the wedges ½ inch apart on a lightly greased baking sheet and sprinkle with sugar. Bake at 425 degrees for 13 to 15 minutes or until golden brown. Cool on the baking sheet for 10 minutes. Remove the scones to a wire rack to cool completely.

Yield: 12 scones

# Harvest Apple Cake

2 cups flour
2 teaspoons baking soda
2 teaspoons cinnamon
¹/2 teaspoon salt
³/4 cup (1¹/2 sticks) unsalted butter, softened
1¹/2 cups sugar
2 eggs
1 teaspoon vanilla extract
4 cups finely chopped peeled Granny Smith apples
(4 or 5 apples)
1 cup walnuts, chopped

Mix the flour, baking soda, cinnamon and salt in a bowl. Beat the butter and sugar in a large bowl until light and fluffy. Add the eggs and vanilla and beat well. Add the dry ingredients and stir until just blended. Fold in the apples and walnuts; the batter will be very stiff. Spread the batter into a greased and floured 9×13-inch glass baking dish. Bake at 350 degrees for 40 to 50 minutes or until a wooden pick inserted in the center comes out clean. Remove to a wire rack to cool completely. Cut into squares to serve.

Yield: 12 servings

*Note:* This is a great breakfast or snack cake!

## Banana Coconut Coffee Cake

1 (2-layer) package Moist Deluxe yellow cake mix
1 (3$\frac{1}{2}$-ounce) package vanilla instant pudding mix
4 eggs
1 cup sour cream
$\frac{1}{2}$ cup canola oil
$\frac{1}{4}$ cup water
$\frac{1}{4}$ cup sugar
1 cup flaked coconut
$\frac{1}{2}$ cup finely chopped pecans
2 large or 3 small bananas, mashed

Combine the cake mix, pudding mix, eggs, sour cream, oil, water
and sugar in a large bowl. Beat with an electric mixer until smooth.
Stir in the coconut, pecans and mashed bananas. Pour the batter
into a large tube pan coated with nonstick cooking spray. Bake at
350 degrees for 50 minutes or until a wooden pick inserted in the
center comes out clean. Cool in the pan for 15 minutes. Remove to
a wire rack to cool completely.

Yield: 12 to 14 servings

# Cranberry Almond Coffee Cake

2 cups flour
1 teaspoon baking powder
1 teaspoon baking soda
1/2 teaspoon salt
1/2 cup (1 stick) butter, softened
1 cup sugar
2 eggs
1 teaspoon almond extract
1 cup sour cream
1 (16-ounce) can whole cranberry sauce
1/2 cup sliced almonds
Confectioners' sugar

Mix the flour, baking powder, baking soda and salt in a bowl. Beat the butter and sugar in a large bowl until light and fluffy. Beat in the eggs and almond extract. Stir in the dry ingredients alternately with the sour cream. Stir until combined, but do not overmix. Pour half the batter into a large bundt pan coated with nonstick cooking spray. Top with half the cranberry sauce and half the almonds. Swirl through the batter gently with a knife to create a marbled effect. Add the remaining batter and top with the remaining cranberry sauce and almonds. Swirl again. Bake at 350 degrees for 55 minutes or until a wooden pick inserted in the center comes out clean. Cool in the pan for 15 to 20 minutes. Remove to a serving plate to cool completely. Dust with confectioners' sugar.

Yield: 16 servings

# Fresh Fruit and Sour Cream Coffee Cake

CRUST
1½ cups flour
½ cup sugar
1½ teaspoons baking powder
½ cup (1 stick) unsalted butter, softened
1 egg
1 teaspoon vanilla extract

TOPPING
2 cups fresh blueberries, raspberries or sliced peaches
2 cups sour cream
2 egg yolks
½ cup sugar
1 teaspoon vanilla extract

*For the crust,* combine the flour, sugar, baking powder, butter, egg and vanilla in a bowl. Beat with an electric mixer at medium speed until crumbly. Press evenly into the bottom and ¾ up the side of a greased 10-inch springform pan.

*For the topping,* arrange the fruit evenly on the crust. Combine the sour cream, egg yolks, sugar and vanilla in a bowl. Beat with an electric mixer at medium speed until blended. Pour over the fruit, spreading to cover all the fruit. Bake at 350 degrees for 1 hour and 10 minutes or until just starting to brown; the topping will not be totally set. Remove to a wire rack and let cool completely. Loosen from the side of the pan with a sharp knife and remove the side. Remove the cake to a serving platter using a large spatula.

Yield: 14 servings

*Note:* If made the night before, refrigerate until ready to serve.

## *Pumpkin Pecan Coffee Cake*

1 teaspoon butter
1/4 cup rolled oats
3 tablespoons packed brown sugar
3 tablespoons chopped pecans
3 tablespoons butter, softened
1/3 cup sugar
1/4 cup packed brown sugar
1 egg
1 1/4 cups flour
1 teaspoon pumpkin pie spice
1 teaspoon baking powder
1/2 teaspoon baking soda
1/2 cup canned pumpkin
1/2 cup low-fat buttermilk

Melt 1 teaspoon butter in a 9-inch round cake pan in the oven. Tilt to coat the pan evenly with melted butter. Mix the oats, 3 tablespoons brown sugar and pecans in a small bowl. Sprinkle evenly over the melted butter in the pan. Combine 3 tablespoons butter, the sugar and 1/4 cup brown sugar in a bowl. Beat with an electric mixer at medium speed for 4 minutes or until well blended. Add the egg and beat well. Mix the flour, pumpkin pie spice, baking powder and baking soda in a bowl. Add to the egg mixture alternately with the pumpkin and buttermilk, beginning and ending with the dry ingredients and beating well after each addition. Spoon the batter evenly over the oat mixture in the pan. Bake at 350 degrees for 40 minutes or until a wooden pick inserted in the center comes out clean. Cool in the pan for 5 to 10 minutes. Invert onto a serving platter and serve warm or at room temperature.

Yield: 8 servings

# Raspberry Cream Cheese Coffee Cake

2¼ cups flour
¾ cup sugar
¾ cup (1½ sticks) chilled unsalted butter, cut into pieces
½ teaspoon baking powder
½ teaspoon baking soda
¼ teaspoon salt
¾ cup sour cream
1 egg
1 teaspoon almond extract
8 ounces cream cheese, softened
¼ cup sugar
1 egg
½ cup raspberry preserves
½ cup sliced almonds

Mix the flour and ¾ cup sugar in a large bowl. Cut in the butter with a pastry blender until crumbly. Remove 1 cup of the mixture and set aside for topping. Add the baking powder, baking soda, salt, sour cream, 1 egg and almond extract to the remaining mixture. Stir to mix well. Spread evenly into the bottom and halfway up the side of a greased 10-inch springform pan, using floured hands. Combine the cream cheese, ¼ cup sugar and 1 egg in a bowl. Beat with an electric mixer until smooth. Spread over the crust in the pan. Top with the raspberry preserves. Add the almonds to the reserved crumb mixture and sprinkle over the preserves. Bake at 350 degrees for 45 to 55 minutes or until the center is set and the crust is golden brown. Remove to a wire rack and let cool completely. Loosen from the side of the pan with a sharp knife and remove the side.

Yield: 12 servings

*Note:* If made the night before, refrigerate until ready to serve.

## Almond Streusel Coffee Cake

1 cup each packed brown sugar and sliced almonds
2¼ cups flour
3 tablespoons butter, melted
2 teaspoons grated orange zest
½ cup (1 stick) unsalted butter, softened
½ cup sugar
3 eggs
½ teaspoon vanilla extract
1 teaspoon each baking powder and baking soda
⅔ cup plus 2½ teaspoons orange juice
½ cup confectioners' sugar

Mix the brown sugar, almonds and ¼ cup of the flour in a bowl. Add the melted butter and 1 teaspoon of the orange zest and stir to mix well. Set aside.

Combine the softened butter and sugar in a large bowl. Beat with an electric mixer at medium speed until light and fluffy. Add the eggs 1 at a time, beating well after each addition. Beat in the remaining orange zest and vanilla. Mix the remaining flour, baking powder and baking soda in a bowl. Beat into the egg mixture at low speed alternately with ⅔ cup of the orange juice, beginning and ending with the dry ingredients. Spoon half the batter into a greased 10-inch tube pan. Sprinkle with half the streusel. Top with the remaining batter and sprinkle with the remaining streusel. Bake at 350 degrees for 30 to 35 minutes or until a wooden pick inserted in the center comes out clean. Remove to a wire rack and let cool in the pan. Invert the cake onto a serving platter when cool. Mix the confectioners' sugar and remaining orange juice in a small bowl until smooth. Drizzle over the cake.

Yield: 16 servings

# Cinnamon Coffee Cake

1 (2-layer) package yellow cake mix with pudding
4 eggs
2/3 cup canola oil
1/3 cup water
1 cup sour cream
1/2 cup packed brown sugar
1 teaspoon cinnamon
2/3 cup chopped pecans (optional)
1 cup confectioners' sugar
2 tablespoons milk
1/2 teaspoon vanilla extract

Beat the cake mix, eggs, oil, water and sour cream in a large bowl with an electric mixer at medium speed until smooth. Pour half the batter into a greased and floured 9×13-inch cake pan. Mix the brown sugar, cinnamon and pecans in a bowl. Sprinkle half over the batter in the pan. Add the remaining batter and top with the remaining brown sugar mixture. Swirl through the batter gently with a knife to create a marbled effect. Bake at 350 degrees for 30 to 35 minutes or until the cake tests done. Remove to a wire rack. Drizzle a mixture of the confectioners' sugar, milk and vanilla over the cake. Let cool completely and cut into squares to serve.

Yield: 16 to 20 servings

# Chocolate Chip Sour Cream Coffee Cake

1/2 cup shortening
1 cup sugar
2 eggs
1 cup sour cream
2 cups flour
1 teaspoon cinnamon
1 teaspoon baking powder
1/2 teaspoon salt
1/2 cup sugar
1 cup chocolate chips
1/2 cup chopped walnuts or pecans

Beat the shortening and 1 cup sugar in a bowl until light and fluffy. Add the eggs and sour cream and beat well. Mix the flour, cinnamon, baking powder and salt in a bowl. Add to the egg mixture and stir until well combined. Spoon half the batter into a greased and floured tube pan. Mix 1/2 cup sugar, the chocolate chips and walnuts in a bowl. Spoon half over the batter. Swirl through the batter gently with a knife to create a marbled effect. Add the remaining batter and top with the remaining chocolate chip mixture. Swirl again. Bake at 350 degrees for 45 minutes or until a wooden pick inserted in the center comes out clean. Remove to a wire rack to cool.

Yield: 12 to 14 servings

*Note:* We would like to thank our friend Lynnette Scofield
at the William Henry Miller Inn in
Ithaca, New York, for this excellent recipe.

# Savory Breakfast Dishes

# Sun-Dried Tomato and Basil Frittata

4 eggs
2 tablespoons grated Parmigiano-Reggiano cheese
1/4 teaspoon kosher salt
Pepper to taste
1/3 cup sun-dried tomatoes packed in oil,
drained and coarsely chopped
2 tablespoons thinly sliced fresh basil
1 1/2 teaspoons butter
1/2 cup chopped yellow onion
Pinch of kosher salt
1 ounce cream cheese, cut into pieces
Hot sauce to taste

Whisk the eggs, Parmigiano-Reggiano cheese and 1/4 teaspoon kosher salt in a bowl. Season with pepper. Stir in the sun-dried tomatoes and basil, reserving a little of each for garnish. Melt the butter in an 8-inch ovenproof skillet over medium-high heat. Add the onion and a pinch of kosher salt. Season with pepper. Sauté for 5 minutes or until the onion is tender. Add the egg mixture and stir gently. Reduce the heat to medium-low. Scatter the pieces of cream cheese on top. Cook for 5 minutes or until set on the bottom and the eggs are 3/4 cooked through, lifting the edges occasionally with an ovenproof spatula and allowing the uncooked eggs to flow under. Place the skillet under a preheated broiler for 1 minute or until the center is set. Slice the frittata in half and place on 2 plates. Garnish with the reserved sun-dried tomatoes and basil. Serve with hot sauce on the side.

Yield: 2 servings

# Three-Mushroom Frittata

2 tablespoons butter
1 cup button mushrooms, sliced
1 cup cremini mushrooms, sliced
1 cup portobello or shiitake mushrooms, sliced
Salt and pepper to taste
2 teaspoons chopped fresh thyme
8 eggs, beaten
2 cups (8 ounces) shredded Vermont sharp
Cheddar cheese

Melt the butter in a 10-inch ovenproof skillet over medium heat.
Add the button mushrooms, cremini mushrooms and portobello
mushrooms. Sauté until the mushrooms are tender. Season with salt
and pepper and stir in the thyme. Increase the heat to medium-high
and add the eggs. Cook until the eggs are almost set, lifting the
edges occasionally with an ovenproof spatula and allowing the
uncooked eggs to flow under. Sprinkle the cheese evenly over the
eggs. Place the skillet under a preheated broiler for 3 minutes
or until the cheese melts and the eggs are fully cooked. Cut into
wedges and serve.

Yield: 4 servings

## Greek Frittata

8 eggs
1 teaspoon Greek seasoning
Salt and pepper to taste
2 tablespoons clarified or regular butter
1/2 cup chopped onion
1 cup frozen spinach, thawed and drained
3/4 cup chopped tomato
1/3 cup feta cheese, crumbled

Beat the eggs and Greek seasoning in a bowl. Season with salt and pepper. Heat the butter in a 10-inch ovenproof skillet over medium heat. Add the onion and sauté until golden brown. Stir in the spinach. Add the egg mixture. Cook until the eggs are almost set, lifting the edges occasionally with an ovenproof spatula and allowing the uncooked eggs to flow under. Sprinkle with the tomato and cheese. Season with pepper. Place the skillet under a preheated broiler for about 1 minute or until the cheese begins to melt and the eggs are fully cooked. Cut into wedges and serve.

Yield: 4 servings

## Bacon, Baby Spinach and Gruyère Omelet

1/2 teaspoon olive oil
1 cup baby spinach, rinsed and stems removed
1 tablespoon butter
3 eggs, beaten
1/4 cup chopped cooked bacon
1/4 cup (1 ounce) shredded Gruyère cheese

Heat the olive oil in a small skillet. Add the spinach and sauté for
1 to 2 minutes or until just wilted. Set aside.

Heat the butter in a 6-inch ovenproof skillet over medium-high heat
for 1 to 2 minutes. Add the eggs. Cook until the eggs are 3/4 cooked
through, lifting the edges occasionally with an ovenproof spatula
and allowing the uncooked eggs to flow under. Spoon the cooked
spinach, bacon and cheese on top of the eggs. Place the skillet
under a preheated broiler until the cheese melts and the eggs are
fully cooked. Fold the omelet in half and slide onto a serving plate.

Yield: 1 serving

# Bacon, Tomato and Mushroom Omelet

6 slices bacon
3/4 cup button mushrooms, sliced
1 large tomato, chopped
1 tablespoon butter
6 eggs, beaten

Cook the bacon in a medium skillet until crisp. Remove to paper towels to drain; crumble. Add the mushrooms to the bacon drippings in the skillet. Sauté until the mushrooms are tender. Add the tomato and cook until thickened and most of the liquid evaporates. Stir in the crumbled bacon. Set aside.

Divide the butter between two 6-inch ovenproof skillets. Heat over medium-high heat for 1 to 2 minutes. Divide the beaten eggs between the skillets. Cook until the eggs are 3/4 cooked through, lifting the edges occasionally with an ovenproof spatula and allowing the uncooked eggs to flow under. Divide the mushroom mixture on top of the eggs. Place the skillets under a preheated broiler until the eggs are fully cooked. Fold the omelets in half and slide onto serving plates.

Yield: 2 servings

# Sausage, Apple and Cheddar Omelet

1½ teaspoons butter
½ large Granny Smith apple, peeled, cored and thinly sliced
⅛ teaspoon cinnamon
Pinch of nutmeg
½ cup sliced or cubed precooked pork breakfast sausage
1½ teaspoons butter
3 eggs, beaten
⅓ cup shredded Vermont sharp Cheddar cheese

Melt 1½ teaspoons butter in a small skillet. Add the apple, cinnamon and nutmeg. Sauté until the apple is tender but firm. Stir in the sausage. Set aside.

Heat 1½ teaspoons butter in a 6-inch ovenproof skillet over medium-high heat for 1 to 2 minutes. Add the eggs. Cook until the eggs are ¾ cooked through, lifting the edges occasionally with an ovenproof spatula and allowing the uncooked eggs to flow under. Spoon the cooked apple mixture on top of the eggs and sprinkle with the cheese. Place the skillet under a preheated broiler until the cheese melts and the eggs are fully cooked. Fold the omelet in half and slide onto a serving plate.

Yield: 1 serving

*Note:* Many guests tell us they never would
have tried this combination on their own, but they love it
once they've tried it.

## Greek Omelet

1 teaspoon olive oil
1 cup fresh spinach, rinsed and stems removed, or
1/2 cup frozen spinach, thawed and drained
1 tablespoon chopped red onion
Splash of dry white wine
1/4 teaspoon Greek seasoning
1 1/2 teaspoons butter
3 eggs, beaten
1/4 cup chopped tomato
1 ounce feta cheese, crumbled

Heat the olive oil in a small skillet. Add the spinach and onion and sauté. Add the wine and Greek seasoning and sauté until the onion is tender. Set aside.

Heat the butter in a 6-inch ovenproof skillet over medium-high heat for 1 to 2 minutes. Add the eggs. Cook until the eggs are 3/4 cooked through, lifting the edges occasionally with an ovenproof spatula and allowing the uncooked eggs to flow under. Spoon the cooked spinach mixture on top of the eggs and sprinkle with the tomato and cheese. Place the skillet under a preheated broiler until the cheese melts and the eggs are fully cooked. Fold the omelet in half and slide onto a serving plate.

Yield: 1 serving

## Spanish Omelet

1 teaspoon olive oil
1/4 cup sliced button mushrooms
1/4 cup chopped tomato
2 tablespoons chopped green bell pepper
1 1/2 teaspoons butter
3 eggs, beaten
2 tablespoons salsa
1/2 teaspoon chopped fresh cilantro

Heat the olive oil in a small skillet. Add the mushrooms, tomato and bell pepper and sauté until the vegetables are tender. Set aside.

Heat the butter in a 6-inch ovenproof skillet over medium-high heat for 1 to 2 minutes. Add the eggs. Cook until the eggs are 3/4 cooked through, lifting the edges occasionally with an ovenproof spatula and allowing the uncooked eggs to flow under. Spoon the cooked vegetables on top of the eggs. Place the skillet under a preheated broiler until the eggs are fully cooked. Fold the omelet in half and slide onto a serving plate. Top with the salsa and cilantro.

Yield: 1 serving

# Smoked Ham and Vermont Cheddar Omelet

3 eggs, beaten
1¹/₂ teaspoons butter
¹/₃ cup chopped smoked ham
¹/₃ cup shredded Vermont sharp Cheddar cheese

Cook the eggs in the butter in a 6-inch ovenproof skillet over medium-high heat until ³/₄ cooked through, lifting the edges to allow the uncooked eggs to flow under. Sprinkle with the ham and cheese. Broil until cooked through. Fold the omelet in half. Slide onto a serving plate.

Yield: 1 serving

# Provençal Omelet

¹/₂ teaspoon olive oil
¹/₂ cup chopped red bell pepper
1 tablespoon butter
6 eggs, beaten
¹/₂ cup drained canned artichoke hearts, quartered
¹/₄ cup sliced green onions
2 ounces goat cheese, crumbled

Heat the olive oil in a small skillet. Add the bell pepper and sauté until tender. Set aside. Divide the butter between two 6-inch ovenproof skillets. Heat over medium-high heat for 1 to 2 minutes. Divide the beaten eggs between the skillets. Cook until the eggs are ³/₄ cooked through, lifting the edges to allow the uncooked eggs to flow under. Sprinkle each with the cooked bell pepper. Top with the remaining ingredients. Broil until cooked through. Fold the omelets in half and slide onto serving plates.

Yield: 2 servings

# Portobello, Red Pepper and Swiss Omelet

1 teaspoon olive oil
1/4 cup chopped portobello mushroom
1/4 cup chopped red bell pepper
1 1/2 teaspoons butter
3 eggs, beaten
1/3 cup shredded Swiss cheese

Heat the olive oil in a small skillet. Add the mushroom and bell pepper and sauté until the vegetables are tender. Set aside.

Heat the butter in a 6-inch ovenproof skillet over medium-high heat for 1 to 2 minutes. Add the eggs. Cook until the eggs are 3/4 cooked through, lifting the edges occasionally with an ovenproof spatula and allowing the uncooked eggs to flow under. Spoon the cooked vegetables on top of the eggs and sprinkle with the cheese. Place the skillet under a preheated broiler until the cheese melts and the eggs are fully cooked. Fold the omelet in half and slide onto a serving plate.

Yield: 1 serving

# Vegetable Medley Omelet

1 teaspoon olive oil
3/4 cup fresh vegetables, such as bell peppers, onion, zucchini,
yellow squash, mushrooms and asparagus
1 1/2 teaspoons butter
3 eggs, beaten
1/4 cup (1 ounce) shredded Vermont sharp
Cheddar cheese

Heat the olive oil in a small skillet. Add the vegetables and sauté until the vegetables are tender-crisp. Set aside.

Heat the butter in a 6-inch ovenproof skillet over medium-high heat for 1 to 2 minutes. Add the eggs. Cook until the eggs are 3/4 cooked through, lifting the edges occasionally with an ovenproof spatula and allowing the uncooked eggs to flow under. Spoon the cooked vegetables on top of the eggs and sprinkle with the cheese. Place the skillet under a preheated broiler until the cheese melts and the eggs are fully cooked. Fold the omelet in half and slide onto a serving plate.

Yield: 1 serving

# Asparagus, Cheddar and Prosciutto Omelet

6 asparagus spears, trimmed of all but the top 2 to 3 inches
3 cups boiling water
1½ teaspoons butter
3 eggs, beaten
2 ounces very thinly sliced prosciutto
¼ cup (1 ounce) shredded Vermont smoked
Cheddar cheese

Cook the asparagus tips in the boiling water in a saucepan for
2 minutes or until just blanched. Drain and rinse quickly under cold
water. Set aside.

Heat the butter in a 6-inch ovenproof skillet over medium-high heat
for 1 to 2 minutes. Add the eggs. Cook until the eggs are ¾ cooked
through, lifting the edges occasionally with an ovenproof spatula
and allowing the uncooked eggs to flow under. Add the asparagus
and prosciutto on top of the eggs and sprinkle with the cheese.
Place the skillet under a preheated broiler until the cheese melts and
the eggs are fully cooked. Fold the omelet in half and slide onto a
serving plate.

Yield: 1 serving

*Note:* Look for thin asparagus spears. They are more tender.

# Apple and Brie Omelet

1¹/2 teaspoons butter
¹/2 large Granny Smith apple, peeled, cored and thinly sliced
¹/8 teaspoon cinnamon
Pinch of nutmeg
1¹/2 teaspoons butter
3 eggs, beaten
3 ounces Brie cheese, rind removed and
cut into small cubes

Melt 1¹/2 teaspoons butter in a small skillet. Add the apple, cinnamon and nutmeg. Sauté until the apple is tender but firm. Set aside.

Heat 1¹/2 teaspoons butter in a 6-inch ovenproof skillet over medium-high heat for 1 to 2 minutes. Add the eggs. Cook until the eggs are ³/4 cooked through, lifting the edges occasionally with an ovenproof spatula and allowing the uncooked eggs to flow under. Add the cheese cubes evenly on top of the eggs. Place the skillet under a preheated broiler until the cheese melts and the eggs are fully cooked. Fold the omelet in half and slide onto a serving plate.

Yield: 1 serving

## Canadian Bacon and Leek Quiche

1 (1-crust) pie pastry
1 tablespoon unsalted butter
1 leek, trimmed, well rinsed and cut crosswise into ¼-inch slices
6 slices Canadian bacon, halved and cut into strips
3 eggs
1½ cups half-and-half
¼ teaspoon salt
¼ teaspoon pepper
6 ounces Gruyère cheese, shredded
1½ teaspoons cornstarch

Fit the pie pastry into a deep-dish glass pie plate. Prick the bottom and side with a fork and trim the edges, if necessary. Bake at 400 degrees for 8 to 10 minutes or until just beginning to brown. Remove to a wire rack and let cool.

Heat the butter in a nonstick skillet over medium-low heat until it begins to bubble. Add the leek and sauté for 8 to 10 minutes or until tender but not brown. Remove to a bowl. Add the Canadian bacon to the skillet and increase the heat to medium-high. Fry for 4 to 6 minutes or until beginning to brown. Add to the cooked leek. Beat the eggs, half-and-half, salt and pepper in a large bowl. Toss the cheese and cornstarch in a bowl. Add to the egg mixture. Add the cooked leek and Canadian bacon and stir gently to mix. Pour into the partially baked pie shell. Bake at 325 degrees for 40 minutes or until the center is set.

Yield: 5 servings

# Savory Ham Quiche

1 (1-crust) pie pastry
1 tablespoon butter
¼ cup chopped onion
8 ounces cream cheese, cut into pieces
¾ cup milk
4 eggs, lightly beaten
1 cup finely chopped ham
1 (2-ounce) jar diced pimento, undrained
¼ teaspoon dried dill weed
⅛ teaspoon pepper

Fit the pie pastry into a deep-dish glass pie plate. Prick the bottom and side with a fork and trim the edges, if necessary. Bake at 400 degrees for 8 to 10 minutes or until just beginning to brown. Remove to a wire rack and let cool.

Melt the butter in a saucepan over medium-high heat. Add the onion and sauté until tender. Add the cream cheese and milk. Cook until the cheese melts, whisking constantly. Whisk ¼ of the hot mixture slowly into the eggs in a large bowl. Whisk the remaining hot mixture into the eggs. Whisk in the ham, pimento, dill weed and pepper. Pour into the partially baked pie shell. Bake at 350 degrees for 35 to 40 minutes or until the center is set.

Yield: 5 servings

## Tomato and Vidalia Onion Quiche

1 (1-crust) pie pastry
1 cup (4 ounces) shredded mozzarella cheese
1 cup (4 ounces) shredded Cheddar cheese
2 tomatoes, seeded and chopped
1 Vidalia onion, thinly sliced
1 teaspoon dried basil,
or 1 tablespoon chopped fresh basil
1/4 teaspoon garlic salt
Cracked pepper to taste
3 eggs
1 cup milk
3 tablespoons grated Parmesan cheese

Fit the pie pastry into a deep-dish glass pie plate. Prick the bottom and side with a fork and trim the edge, if necessary. Bake at 400 degrees for 8 to 10 minutes or until just beginning to brown. Remove to a wire rack and let cool.

Sprinkle the mozzarella cheese and Cheddar cheese over the bottom of the pie shell. Layer the tomatoes and onion on top of the cheese. Sprinkle with the basil and garlic salt. Season with cracked pepper. Beat the eggs and milk in a bowl. Pour over the layers in the partially baked pie shell and sprinkle with the Parmesan cheese. Bake at 350 degrees for 45 to 50 minutes or until the center is set.

Yield: 5 servings

## Italian Vegetable Quiche

1 (1-crust) pie pastry
2 tablespoons olive oil
1½ cups chopped onions
1 garlic clove, minced
¾ cup sliced zucchini
1 tablespoon chopped fresh basil, or 1 teaspoon dried basil
¼ teaspoon salt
¾ cup (3 ounces) shredded mozzarella cheese
⅓ cup grated Parmesan cheese
¼ cup sliced black olives
4 eggs
1 cup milk
¼ teaspoon dry mustard
1 tablespoon flour
1 tomato, thinly sliced or chopped

Fit the pie pastry into a deep-dish glass pie plate. Prick the bottom and side with a fork and trim the edge, if necessary. Bake at 400 degrees for 8 to 10 minutes or until just beginning to brown. Remove to a wire rack and let cool.

Heat the olive oil in a medium skillet. Add the onions, garlic and zucchini and sauté until the vegetables are tender. Stir in the basil and salt and set aside.

Mix the mozzarella cheese and Parmesan cheese in a bowl. Layer half the cheese mixture, onion mixture and olives in the pie shell. Whisk the eggs, milk, dry mustard and flour in a bowl. Pour over the layers and sprinkle with the remaining cheese mixture. Arrange the tomato on top of the cheese. Bake at 375 degrees for 40 to 45 minutes or until the center is set.

Yield: 5 servings

## Summer Vegetable Quiche

1 (1-crust) pie pastry
2 tablespoons olive oil
½ red bell pepper, chopped
½ green bell pepper, chopped
2 garlic cloves, minced
¼ to ½ cup chopped zucchini
2 tablespoons chopped fresh basil, or 1 tablespoon dried basil
4 eggs
1 cup half-and-half
1 teaspoon salt
½ teaspoon pepper
1 cup (4 ounces) shredded sharp Cheddar cheese
1 cup (4 ounces) shredded mozzarella cheese
1 medium to large tomato, chopped
⅓ cup grated Parmesan cheese

Fit the pie pastry into a deep-dish glass pie plate. Prick the bottom and side with a fork and trim the edge, if necessary. Bake at 400 degrees for 8 to 10 minutes or until just beginning to brown. Remove to a wire rack and let cool.

Heat the olive oil in a medium skillet. Add the red bell pepper, green bell pepper, garlic, zucchini and basil and sauté until the vegetables are tender. Set aside.

Whisk the eggs, half-and-half, salt and pepper in a large bowl. Stir in the cooked vegetables, Cheddar cheese and mozzarella cheese. Pour into the partially baked pie shell. Top with the chopped tomato and press into the filling. Sprinkle with the Parmesan cheese. Bake at 375 degrees for 45 minutes or until the center is set.

Yield: 5 servings

# Bacon, Tomato and Cheddar Strata

6 slices bacon
1 cup very thinly sliced onion
2 garlic cloves, minced
8 cups cubed white bread
8 ounces Cheddar cheese, shredded
3 large tomatoes, seeded and chopped
4 eggs
3 egg whites
2 cups milk
1/4 cup fresh basil, thinly sliced
1/4 teaspoon each salt and pepper
1/4 teaspoon thyme

Cook the bacon in a medium skillet until crisp. Remove to paper towels to drain; crumble. Add the onion to the bacon drippings in the skillet. Sauté for 4 minutes. Add the garlic and sauté for 1 minute or until the onion is tender. Remove from the heat and stir in the cooked bacon.

Arrange half the bread cubes in a 9×13-inch baking dish coated with nonstick cooking spray. Top with 1/3 of the cheese, half the onion mixture and half the tomatoes. Whisk the eggs, egg whites, milk, basil, salt, pepper and thyme in a bowl. Pour half over the layers in the baking dish. Top with the remaining bread cubes, 1/2 of the remaining cheese, the remaining onion mixture and the remaining tomatoes. Pour the remaining milk mixture over the layers. Cover and chill for at least 1 hour and up to 18 hours. Bake, uncovered, at 325 degrees for 55 minutes. Sprinkle with the remaining 1/3 of the cheese and bake for 5 minutes longer or until the cheese melts. Let stand for 5 minutes before cutting into squares to serve.

Yield: 8 servings

## Sausage and Vermont Cheddar Strata

12 ounces ground hot pork breakfast sausage
12 ounces ground regular pork breakfast sausage
6 slices potato bread, crusts removed
4 eggs
2½ cups half-and-half
1 teaspoon sage
¾ teaspoon kosher salt
¼ teaspoon pepper
2 cups (8 ounces) shredded Vermont extra-sharp
Cheddar cheese
2 tablespoons chopped fresh flat-leaf parsley

Heat a large skillet over medium-high heat. Add the hot sausage and regular sausage. Cook for 7 minutes or until well browned, stirring occasionally to break up the sausage. Remove to paper towels to drain.

Arrange the bread slices in the bottom of a 9×13-inch baking dish coated with nonstick cooking spray. Top with the cooked sausage. Whisk the eggs, half-and-half, sage, kosher salt and pepper in a bowl. Pour over the layers in the baking dish. Sprinkle with the cheese. Bake at 350 degrees for 30 minutes or until set in the middle; do not overbake. Let stand for 15 to 20 minutes before cutting into squares. Sprinkle each square with chopped parsley just before serving.

Yield: 8 servings

# Poached Eggs with Asiago Cheese Sauce

2 tablespoons butter
2 tablespoons flour
½ cup chicken broth
½ cup heavy cream
½ cup (2 ounces) grated asiago cheese
2 English muffins, split, toasted and buttered
4 slices smoked ham
4 eggs
Freshly ground pepper

Melt the butter in a small saucepan. Stir in the flour. Cook over medium-high heat for 1 minute, stirring constantly. Whisk in the chicken broth and heavy cream. Cook until the sauce is thickened and bubbly, whisking constantly. Stir in the cheese. Cook until the cheese melts, whisking constantly. Remove from the heat and cover to keep warm.

Arrange the buttered muffin halves on a baking sheet. Top each with a slice of smoked ham. Broil 3 inches from the heat source for 2 minutes; keep warm.

Bring ½ inch of water to a boil in a large skillet. Reduce the heat to medium-high. Crack the eggs 1 at a time onto a small plate. Slide each egg into the simmering water. Cook for 4 to 6 minutes, basting the eggs occasionally with simmering water. Remove the eggs with a slotted spoon and dab excess water with a paper towel. Place 1 egg on top of each ham-topped muffin half. Spoon the cheese sauce over and sprinkle with pepper.

Yield: 2 servings

## Denver Scramble

1 teaspoon butter
1/4 cup chopped red bell pepper
1/4 cup chopped green bell pepper
1/4 cup chopped onion
1/4 cup chopped smoked ham
1 teaspoon butter
4 eggs, beaten
1/2 cup (2 ounces) shredded Vermont sharp Cheddar cheese

Melt 1 teaspoon butter in a small skillet. Add the red bell pepper, green bell pepper and onion. Sauté until the vegetables are tender. Stir in the ham. Set aside.

Heat 1 teaspoon butter in a medium ovenproof skillet over medium-high heat. Add the eggs. Cook until the eggs are 3/4 cooked through, stirring often with an ovenproof spatula. Stir in the sautéed vegetables and cheese. Place the skillet under a preheated broiler until the cheese melts and the eggs are fully cooked.

Yield: 2 servings

## Asparagus Breakfast Bake

1 cup (1-inch pieces) fresh asparagus
4 cups boiling water
8 ounces Gruyère cheese, shredded
1/4 cup (1/2 stick) butter, cut into small pieces
1 cup heavy cream
1 1/2 teaspoons dry mustard
1/2 teaspoon salt
Dash of pepper
12 eggs, lightly beaten

Cook the asparagus in the boiling water in a saucepan for 1 to 2 minutes or until just blanched. Drain and rinse quickly under cold water. Set aside.

Spread the cheese evenly in a 9×13-inch baking dish coated with nonstick cooking spray. Dot with the butter. Whisk the heavy cream, dry mustard, salt and pepper in a bowl. Pour half over the cheese in the baking dish. Pour the beaten eggs into the dish and top with the remaining cream mixture. Sprinkle with the asparagus pieces and press into the mixture. Bake at 350 degrees for 30 minutes or until the center is set.

Yield: 8 to 10 servings

## Baked Eggs Florentine

9 eggs
2 cups cottage cheese
2 cups (8 ounces) shredded Swiss cheese
8 ounces feta cheese, crumbled
1/4 cup (1/2 stick) butter, melted
2 (10-ounce) packages frozen chopped spinach,
thawed and well drained
1 teaspoon nutmeg

Beat the eggs lightly in a large bowl. Add the cottage cheese, Swiss cheese, feta cheese and butter and mix well. Stir in the spinach and nutmeg. Pour into a greased 9×13-inch baking pan. Bake at 350 degrees for 1 hour or until a knife inserted in the center comes out clean.

Yield: 8 servings

*Note:* This casserole can be prepared the night before. Cover and refrigerate. Let stand at room temperature for 20 to 30 minutes before baking.

## Southwestern Breakfast Casserole

4 (4-ounce) cans chopped green chiles
6 soft flour tortillas, cut into 1/4-inch strips
1 pound turkey or pork sausage, cooked, drained and crumbled
2 cups (8 ounces) shredded Monterey Jack cheese
10 eggs
1/2 cup milk
1 teaspoon dried onion flakes
1/2 teaspoon salt
1/2 teaspoon pepper
1/2 teaspoon garlic salt
1/2 teaspoon cumin
2 large tomatoes, chopped
Salsa and sour cream for garnish

Layer half the chiles, half the tortilla strips, half the cooked sausage and half the cheese in a greased 9×13-inch baking dish. Repeat the layers using the remaining chiles, tortilla strips, cooked sausage and cheese. Beat the eggs, milk, onion flakes, salt, pepper, garlic salt and cumin in a large bowl. Pour evenly over the layers in the baking dish. Arrange the chopped tomatoes evenly on top. Bake at 350 degrees for 50 to 60 minutes or until the center is set. Cut into squares. Serve hot, topped with salsa and a dollop of sour cream.

Yield: 8 servings

*Note:* This casserole can be prepared the night before. Cover tightly and refrigerate. Bake for 5 to 10 minutes longer if chilled when placed in the oven. We would like to thank our friend Yvonne Martin at the White Oak Inn in Danville, Ohio, for this recipe.

# Sweet Breakfast Dishes

# Strawberry Blueberry Crepes

1/2 cup each cold water and cold milk
2 eggs
1 cup flour
1/4 teaspoon salt
2 tablespoons butter, melted
8 ounces cream cheese, softened
1 cup sour cream
1/3 cup confectioners' sugar
1 cup fresh strawberries
1/4 cup sugar
2 1/2 cups lightly sweetened hulled strawberries and blueberries
Whipped cream and fresh mint leaves for garnish

Process the water, milk, eggs, flour, salt and melted butter in a blender until smooth. Chill for 2 to 3 hours. Heat a lightly oiled skillet or crepe pan. Pour 3 to 4 tablespoons of batter into the pan. Tilt the pan to form a 6-inch crepe. Cook until light brown on the bottom and remove to a wire rack to cool. Repeat with the remaining batter. Beat the cream cheese, sour cream and confectioners' sugar in a bowl with an electric mixer until smooth. Crush 1 cup strawberries with the sugar in a bowl. Stir until the sugar dissolves. Spoon 3 to 4 tablespoons of the cream cheese mixture on each crepe. Roll up and place seam side down in a baking pan. Bake the filled crepes at 350 degrees for 5 to 7 minutes. Place 2 crepes on each of 8 serving plates. Spoon the strawberry mixture on the crepes. Sprinkle with 2 1/2 cups strawberries and blueberries. Top with whipped cream and garnish with mint.

Yield: 8 servings

*Note:* The crepes can be made the night before and refrigerated or frozen for longer periods. Stack between layers of waxed paper or parchment paper. Bring to room temperature before assembling.

## Baked Apple Pancake

3/4 cup flour
3 tablespoons sugar
1/4 teaspoon salt
3 eggs
3/4 cup light cream
2 tablespoons butter, melted
2 large apples, peeled, cored and thinly sliced
2 tablespoons packed brown sugar
1/2 teaspoon cinnamon
2 tablespoons butter, melted
Confectioners' sugar for dusting
Pure Vermont maple syrup

Mix the flour, sugar, salt, eggs, cream and 2 tablespoons melted butter in a mixing bowl until smooth. Heat a 10-inch ovenproof skillet sprayed with nonstick cooking spray over medium heat. Pour in the batter. Cook until set. Remove from the heat and arrange the apples on top of the pancake to completely cover the surface. Mix the brown sugar and cinnamon in a small bowl. Sprinkle over the apples and drizzle with 2 tablespoons melted butter. Bake at 400 degrees for 6 to 8 minutes. Cut into 4 wedges and place on serving plates. Dust with confectioners' sugar and serve with warm maple syrup.

Yield: 4 servings

# Blueberry Buttermilk Pancakes

1¹/₃ cups all-purpose flour
¹/₄ cup whole wheat flour
1 tablespoon sugar
³/₄ teaspoon baking powder
³/₄ teaspoon baking soda
1¹/₂ cups buttermilk
2 eggs, at room temperature
3 tablespoons butter, melted
2 cups fresh blueberries
Confectioners' sugar for dusting
Pure Vermont maple syrup

Mix the all-purpose flour, whole wheat flour, sugar, baking powder and baking soda in a bowl. Whisk the buttermilk, eggs and melted butter in a small bowl. Add to the dry ingredients and stir until smooth. Fold in the blueberries. Pour ¹/₄ cup at a time onto a medium-hot greased griddle. Turn when bubbles appear on the surface and the edges look dry. Cook until golden brown. Place 3 pancakes on each of 4 serving plates. Dust with confectioners' sugar and serve with warm maple syrup.

Yield: 4 servings

*Variation:* You may substitute bananas, raspberries or strawberries for the blueberries.

## Cinnamon Pancakes

1¼ cups flour
2 tablespoons sugar
1 teaspoon baking powder
½ teaspoon baking soda
½ teaspoon salt
½ teaspoon cinnamon
¼ teaspoon nutmeg
1 egg
1¼ cups buttermilk
2 tablespoons canola oil
Confectioners' sugar for dusting
Pure Vermont maple syrup

Mix the flour, sugar, baking powder, baking soda, salt, cinnamon and nutmeg in a large bowl. Beat the egg, buttermilk and oil in a small bowl. Add to the dry ingredients and stir until just moistened. Pour ¼ cup at a time onto a medium-hot greased griddle. Turn when bubbles appear on the surface and the edges look dry. Cook until golden brown. Place 3 pancakes on each of 3 serving plates. Dust with confectioners' sugar and serve with warm maple syrup.

Yield: 3 servings

## Gingerbread Pancakes

1 cup all-purpose flour
1 cup whole wheat flour
1 tablespoon baking powder
1/2 teaspoon salt
1/2 teaspoon cinnamon
1/4 teaspoon nutmeg
1/4 teaspoon ginger
2 tablespoons packed dark brown sugar
1/2 cup molasses
2 egg yolks
3 tablespoons butter, melted
1 1/2 cups milk
2 egg whites
Confectioners' sugar for dusting
Pure Vermont maple syrup

Mix the all-purpose flour, whole wheat flour, baking powder, salt, cinnamon, nutmeg, ginger and brown sugar in a large bowl. Beat the molasses, egg yolks, melted butter and milk in a bowl. Add to the dry ingredients and stir gently to combine. Beat the egg whites in a small bowl until stiff peaks form. Fold gently into the batter. Pour 1/4 cup at a time onto a hot greased griddle. Cook until golden brown, turning once. Place 3 pancakes on each of 8 serving plates. Dust with confectioners' sugar and serve with warm maple syrup.

Yield: 8 servings

## Banana Oat Griddlecakes

3 egg whites
2 ripe bananas, mashed
1/2 cup milk
2 tablespoons vegetable oil
3/4 cup rolled oats
3/4 cup whole wheat flour
1 teaspoon baking powder
1 teaspoon baking soda
1 teaspoon cinnamon
Confectioners' sugar for dusting
Pure Vermont maple syrup

Beat the egg whites in a large bowl until soft peaks form. Stir in the mashed bananas. Stir in the milk and oil. Mix the oats, whole wheat flour, baking powder, baking soda and cinnamon in a bowl. Add to the banana mixture and stir until just combined. Drop spoonfuls of batter onto a hot greased griddle, spreading with the back of a spoon. Turn when bubbles appear on the surface and the edges look dry. Cook until golden brown. Place 3 pancakes on each of 4 serving plates. Dust with confectioners' sugar and serve with warm maple syrup.

Yield: 4 servings

# Oatmeal Griddlecakes with Cider Sauce

### APPLE CIDER SAUCE
1/2 cup sugar
2 tablespoons cornstarch
1/4 teaspoon each nutmeg and cinnamon
2 cups apple cider
2 tablespoons lemon juice
1/4 cup (1/2 stick) butter

### OATMEAL GRIDDLECAKES
1 cup each rolled oats and whole wheat flour
1/4 cup each wheat germ and nonfat dry milk powder
1 teaspoon baking soda
1/4 teaspoon salt
1 tablespoon packed brown sugar
2 eggs
2 cups buttermilk
1/4 cup (1/2 stick) butter, melted
Confectioners' sugar for dusting

*For the cider sauce,* bring a mixture of the sugar, cornstarch, nutmeg, cinnamon, apple cider and lemon juice to a boil in a saucepan over medium heat. Boil for 1 minute, stirring constantly. Add the butter and cook until the butter melts, stirring constantly. Keep warm.

*For the griddlecakes,* mix the first 7 ingredients in a large bowl. Mix the eggs, buttermilk and butter in a bowl. Add to the dry ingredients and stir until well mixed. Pour 1/4 cup at a time onto a medium-hot greased griddle. Turn when bubbles appear on the surface and the edges look dry. Cook until golden brown. Place 3 pancakes on each of 8 serving plates. Dust with confectioners' sugar and serve with Apple Cider Sauce.

Yield: 8 servings

## Orange Pecan Waffles

1 cup flour
1 tablespoon sugar
1 teaspoon baking powder
1/8 teaspoon salt
1/8 teaspoon grated orange zest
1 egg yolk, at room temperature
3/4 cup orange juice
1/4 cup (1/2 stick) butter, melted and cooled
1/4 to 1/3 cup finely chopped pecans
1 egg white, at room temperature
Confectioners' sugar for dusting
Grated orange zest for garnish
Pure Vermont maple syrup

Mix the flour, sugar, baking powder, salt and 1/8 teaspoon orange zest in a bowl. Mix the egg yolk, orange juice and melted butter in a bowl. Add to the dry ingredients and stir until just combined. Fold in the pecans. Beat the egg white in a small bowl until stiff. Fold into the batter until just combined; do not overmix. Ladle 1/4 of the batter onto a heated waffle iron, spreading with the back of the ladle almost to the edges. Close the waffle iron and cook until golden brown and crisp. Repeat with the remaining batter. Cut the waffles into sections and arrange on 4 serving plates. Dust with confectioners' sugar, garnish with grated orange zest and serve with warm maple syrup.

Yield: 4 servings

*Note:* If using a Belgian waffle iron, this recipe
makes 2 waffles instead of 4.

# Pumpkin Waffles

½ cup flour
¾ cup rolled or quick-cooking oats
1 tablespoon packed dark brown sugar
1 teaspoon baking powder
¼ teaspoon pumpkin pie spice
⅛ teaspoon salt
1 egg yolk, at room temperature
½ cup canned pumpkin
⅓ cup milk
¼ cup (½ stick) butter, melted and cooled
¼ cup chopped walnuts or pecans (optional)
1 egg white, at room temperature
Confectioners' sugar for dusting
Pure Vermont maple syrup

Mix the flour, oats, brown sugar, baking powder, pumpkin pie spice and salt in a bowl. Mix the egg yolk, pumpkin, milk and melted butter in a bowl. Add to the dry ingredients and stir until just combined. Fold in the walnuts. Beat the egg white in a small bowl until stiff. Fold into the batter until just combined; do not overmix. Ladle ⅓ of the batter onto a heated waffle iron, spreading with the back of the ladle almost to the edges. Close the waffle iron and cook until dark brown and crisp. Repeat with the remaining batter. Cut the waffles into sections and arrange on 3 serving plates. Dust with confectioners' sugar and serve with warm maple syrup.

Yield: 3 servings

*Note:* If using a Belgian waffle iron, this recipe makes 2 waffles instead of 3. Cook these waffles a little dark so they are nice and crisp on the outside.

# Blueberry Raspberry French Toast Bake

12 slices French bread, cubed
16 ounces cream cheese, cut into small cubes and softened
1 cup each fresh blueberries and red raspberries
12 eggs
1/3 cup pure Vermont maple syrup
2 cups milk
1 cup each sugar and water
2 tablespoons cornstarch
1 tablespoon butter
Confectioners' sugar for dusting

Arrange half the bread cubes in a 9×13-inch baking dish coated with nonstick cooking spray. Scatter the cubes of cream cheese on top and sprinkle with 1/2 cup each of the blueberries and raspberries. Top with the remaining bread cubes. Beat the eggs, maple syrup and milk in a large bowl. Pour evenly over the layers in the baking dish. Cover with foil and chill overnight. Let stand at room temperature for 15 minutes. Bake, covered, at 350 degrees for 30 minutes. Remove the foil and bake for 30 minutes longer or until puffed. Combine the sugar, water and cornstarch in a saucepan. Cook over medium-high heat until thickened, stirring often. Add the remaining blueberries and raspberries. Bring to a boil, stirring often. Reduce the heat to medium and add the butter. Cook until the butter melts, stirring constantly. Cut the French toast bake into 8 squares and place on serving plates. Top with the sauce and dust with confectioners' sugar.

Yield: 8 servings

*Note:* This recipe was given to us by former innkeeper Jane Savage. She and her husband, David, sometimes watch over the Inn for us when we are away in the off-season or if family business calls us away from the Inn. This recipe is a staff favorite, and we love to make it when fresh berries are in season.

## Orange Crème Stuffed French Toast

8 ounces cream cheese, softened
1/4 cup confectioners' sugar
1 rounded tablespoon sour cream
2 teaspoons vanilla extract
Grated zest of 1 orange
1 loaf day-old Italian bread
6 eggs
1 1/2 cups milk
1/2 teaspoon vanilla extract
1 teaspoon cinnamon
1/2 teaspoon nutmeg
Confectioners' sugar and nutmeg for dusting
Orange slices for garnish
Pure Vermont maple syrup

Combine the cream cheese, 1/4 cup confectioners' sugar, sour cream, 2 teaspoons vanilla and orange zest in a bowl. Beat until well mixed. Cover and chill overnight to allow the flavors to blend.

Cut the bread into 1 1/2-inch-thick slices. Cut a pocket in each slice and fill with the cream cheese mixture. Beat the eggs, milk, 1/2 teaspoon vanilla, cinnamon and 1/2 teaspoon nutmeg in a large bowl. Dip the stuffed bread slices into the egg mixture, allowing the bread to become saturated. Cook the French toast on a hot greased griddle until golden brown, turning once. Place on serving plates. Dust with confectioners' sugar and a little nutmeg and garnish with orange slices. Serve with warm maple syrup.

Yield: 6 to 8 servings

*Note:* Make the filling the day before and finish the recipe in the morning.

# Peaches and Cream Stuffed French Toast

8 ounces cream cheese, softened
1/2 cup sour cream
1/4 cup confectioners' sugar, or to taste
3 ripe peaches, peeled, pitted and sliced
1 loaf home-style bakery bread, such as honey-oat
7 eggs
3/4 cup milk
1/4 cup sugar
1 1/2 teaspoons vanilla extract
1 teaspoon nutmeg
Confectioners' sugar for dusting
Pure Vermont maple syrup

Combine the cream cheese, sour cream and 1/4 cup confectioners' sugar in a bowl. Beat until well mixed. Fold in the sliced peaches. Cut the bread into 1-inch-thick slices, discarding the end pieces. Spread the cream cheese mixture on half the bread slices and top each with another slice of bread. Cut each sandwich diagonally in half with a serrated knife. Beat the eggs, milk, sugar, vanilla and nutmeg in a large bowl. Dip the triangles into the egg mixture, allowing the bread to become saturated. Cook the French toast on a medium-hot greased griddle until golden brown, turning once. Place 2 triangles on each of 6 serving plates. Dust with confectioners' sugar and serve with warm maple syrup.

Yield: 6 servings

*Note:* Very decadent!

# Crème Brûlée French Toast

1 cup packed dark brown sugar
1/2 cup (1 stick) unsalted butter
1/4 cup pure Vermont maple syrup
8 (1/2-inch-thick) slices Italian bread
4 eggs
1 cup milk
1 teaspoon vanilla extract
Confectioners' sugar for dusting
1 1/4 cups fresh raspberries

Combine the brown sugar, butter and maple syrup in a saucepan. Heat slowly to a gentle boil, stirring often. Cook until the mixture almost lifts from the side of the pan, stirring often. Pour immediately into a 9×13-inch baking pan coated with nonstick cooking spray, making sure to distribute evenly over the bottom of the pan. Position the bread slices on top of the sticky syrup immediately, squeezing to fit, if necessary. Beat the eggs, milk and vanilla in a bowl. Pour over the bread slices. Cover the pan with plastic wrap and chill overnight.

Bake at 350 degrees for 25 minutes; do not overbake, or the syrup mixture will become hard. Flip 2 slices syrup side up onto each of 4 serving plates. Dust with confectioners' sugar and top with a handful of raspberries.

Yield: 4 servings

*Note:* Make this the night before and refrigerate.
Bake it in the morning.

## Cinnamon French Toast

7 eggs
3/4 cup milk
1/4 cup sugar
1 tablespoon cinnamon
1 1/2 teaspoons vanilla extract
1 loaf home-style bakery bread, such as honey-oat or
cinnamon-swirl
Confectioners' sugar for dusting
Pure Vermont maple syrup

Beat the eggs, milk, sugar, cinnamon and vanilla in a large bowl.
Cut the bread into 1-inch-thick slices, discarding the end pieces.
Cut each slice diagonally in half with a serrated knife. Dip the
triangles into the egg mixture, allowing the bread to become
saturated. Cook the French toast on a medium-hot greased griddle
until golden brown, turning once. Place 3 triangles on each of
6 serving plates. Dust with confectioners' sugar and serve with
warm maple syrup.

Yield: 6 servings

*Note:* An all-time favorite here at the Inn!

## Eggnog French Toast

8 eggs
1¹/2 cups eggnog
1 teaspoon nutmeg
¹/2 teaspoon cinnamon
1 tablespoon dark rum (optional, or to taste)
1 loaf Italian bread, cut into 1-inch-thick slices
Confectioners' sugar and nutmeg for dusting
Pure Vermont maple syrup

Beat the eggs, eggnog, 1 teaspoon nutmeg, cinnamon and rum in a large bowl. Dip the bread slices into the egg mixture, allowing the bread to become saturated. Cook the French toast on a medium-hot greased griddle until golden brown, turning once. Fan out 3 slices on each of 6 serving plates. Dust with confectioners' sugar and a little nutmeg. Serve with warm maple syrup.

Yield: 6 servings

*Note:* Nice for the holiday season!

# Hors d'Oeuvre

# *Meatballs in Creamy Mushroom Sauce*

### MEATBALLS
2 teaspoons olive oil
1 small onion, finely chopped
1 garlic clove, minced
1 slice firm white bread, torn into pieces
1/3 cup milk
8 ounces lean ground pork
8 ounces ground chuck
1 egg, beaten
1 1/2 teaspoons salt
1/2 teaspoon pepper
1/4 teaspoon nutmeg

### SAUCE
2 tablespoons butter
3 shallots, minced
8 ounces button mushrooms, halved
2 tablespoons good-quality brandy
1/3 cup dry red wine
3 tablespoons heavy cream
1 1/2 cups brown beef gravy (purchased or homemade)
1 1/2 teaspoons chopped fresh thyme leaves, or
1/2 teaspoon dried thyme
Salt and pepper to taste

*For the meatballs,* heat the olive oil in a medium skillet over medium heat. Add the onion and sauté for 3 minutes or until softened but not brown. Add the garlic and sauté for 1 minute. Remove from the heat and let cool. Soak the bread in the milk in a small bowl. Combine the ground pork, ground chuck, egg, salt, pepper, nutmeg, cooled onion mixture and bread with liquid in a large bowl. Stir to mix well. Form into 1-inch meatballs. Arrange on 2 baking sheets lined with nonstick foil. Bake at 450 degrees for 8 to 10 minutes or until brown and cooked through, shaking the pans occasionally to rotate the meatballs. Let cool. Cover and chill until ready to serve.

*For the sauce,* melt the butter in a very large skillet over medium heat. Add the shallots and sauté for 2 minutes or until softened but not brown. Add the mushrooms and sauté for 3 to 5 minutes or until the liquid evaporates. Add the brandy and ignite immediately with a long-handled match. Add the wine when the flames subside. Bring to a boil and cook for 4 to 5 minutes or until reduced by half. Whisk in the heavy cream and gravy and bring to a boil. Cook for 5 minutes or until the sauce is just thick enough to coat the back of a spoon. Stir in the thyme and season with salt and pepper. Add the chilled meatballs and cook for 5 minutes or until the meatballs are heated through. Remove to a chafing dish and serve.

Yield: 10 to 12 servings

*Note:* The meatballs may be made up to 24 hours in advance and kept chilled until ready to add to the sauce.

# Chinese Meatballs with Pineapple Sauce

1 pound ground beef
3/4 cup finely chopped celery
1/4 cup finely chopped almonds
1 tablespoon finely chopped fresh gingerroot
1 garlic clove, minced
1 teaspoon salt
1/2 cup bread crumbs
3 tablespoons soy sauce
2 eggs, beaten
1/2 cup sugar
3 tablespoons cornstarch
1 cup chicken broth
1/2 cup white vinegar
1/2 cup pineapple juice
1/2 green bell pepper, cut into strips
1 cup pineapple chunks

Combine the ground beef, celery, almonds, gingerroot, garlic and salt in a large bowl. Stir to mix well. Add the bread crumbs, 1 tablespoon of the soy sauce and eggs and mix well. Shape into walnut-size balls. Arrange the meatballs on a foil-lined baking pan. Bake at 350 degrees for 20 minutes or until brown and cooked through, turning once during baking. Drain on paper towels. Chill until ready to use.

Combine the sugar and cornstarch in a large saucepan. Stir in the chicken broth, vinegar and remaining soy sauce. Stir until smooth. Stir in the pineapple juice. Cook over medium heat until thickened and clear, stirring constantly. Add the bell pepper and pineapple and simmer for 2 minutes. Add the meatballs to the sauce and simmer until the meatballs are heated though. Serve in a chafing dish.

Yield: 10 to 12 servings

## Chinese Chicken Wings

1/2 cup soy sauce
1/2 cup dry sherry
1/4 cup sugar
3 garlic cloves, minced
1 tablespoon grated fresh gingerroot
Dash of crushed red pepper
2 pounds chicken wings

Mix the soy sauce, sherry, sugar, garlic, gingerroot and crushed red pepper in a large bowl. Add the chicken wings and stir to coat. Cover and marinate in the refrigerator for several hours. Remove the wings to a baking sheet lined with nonstick foil. Discard the marinade. Bake at 375 degrees for 40 minutes. Increase the oven temperature to 475 degrees and bake for 10 minutes longer to make the wings crispy.

Yield: 6 servings

*Note:* If the chicken wings are purchased fresh, cut them at the joint and discard the wing tips. If the chicken wings are purchased frozen, thaw them overnight in the refrigerator. Frozen wings usually come with the wing tips removed.

# Walnut Chicken Nuggets with Plum Sauce

### PLUM DIPPING SAUCE
1 cup plum preserves or jam
1 tablespoon ketchup
2 teaspoons grated lemon zest
1 tablespoon lemon juice
2 teaspoons cider vinegar
1/2 teaspoon ginger
1/2 teaspoon anise seeds, crushed
1/4 teaspoon dry mustard
1/4 teaspoon cinnamon
1/8 teaspoon ground cloves
1/8 teaspoon hot sauce

### NUGGETS
1 1/4 pounds boneless skinless chicken breasts,
cut into bite-size pieces
1 tablespoon dry sherry
2 to 2 1/2 cups finely chopped walnuts
1 teaspoon salt
1/8 teaspoon pepper
2 egg whites
1/4 cup cornstarch
Vegetable oil for frying

*For the sauce,* cook the plum preserves in a small skillet over medium heat until melted, stirring often. Stir in the ketchup, lemon zest, lemon juice, vinegar, ginger, anise, dry mustard, cinnamon, cloves and hot sauce. Bring to a boil. Cook for 1 minute, stirring constantly. Set aside.

*For the nuggets,* combine the chicken and sherry in a small bowl. Stir to coat. Mix the walnuts, salt and pepper in a shallow bowl. Beat the egg whites in a mixing bowl with an electric mixer at high speed until foamy. Add the cornstarch and beat at high speed until stiff peaks form.

Heat 2 inches of oil to 350 degrees in a large heavy skillet. Press 1/3 of the chicken pieces between layers of paper towels to remove excess moisture. Dip the chicken pieces in the beaten egg white mixture and then roll in the walnut mixture to coat. Fry in the hot oil until golden brown and cooked through. Drain on paper towels. Repeat with the remaining chicken, egg white mixture and walnut mixture. Place the hot chicken nuggets in a chafing dish and serve with the Plum Dipping Sauce on the side.

Yield: 8 servings

## Moroccan Chicken Wings

5 pounds chicken wings
1/2 cup fresh lemon juice
8 garlic cloves, minced
1³/4 cups flour
2 tablespoons salt
2 tablespoons ground coriander
2 tablespoons ground cumin
2 tablespoons cinnamon
2 tablespoons paprika
1 tablespoon cayenne pepper
1¹/2 teaspoons black pepper
1/2 cup olive oil

Combine the chicken wings, lemon juice and garlic in a large bowl. Toss gently to coat. Combine the flour, salt, coriander, cumin, cinnamon, paprika, cayenne pepper and black pepper in a resealable plastic bag. Seal the bag and shake to mix. Remove the wings a few at a time from the lemon juice marinade to the bag. Discard the lemon juice marinade. Seal the bag and shake to coat the wings with the flour mixture. Place the wings on a 10×15-inch baking pan lined with nonstick foil. Brush with the olive oil. Bake at 400 degrees for 30 minutes or until cooked through. Serve with ranch salad dressing on the side, if desired.

Yield: 12 servings

*Note:* If the chicken wings are purchased fresh, cut them at the joint and discard the wing tips. If the chicken wings are purchased frozen, thaw them overnight in the refrigerator. Frozen wings usually come with the wing tips removed.

# Jamaican Jerk Pork Tenderloin

2 cups coarsely chopped green onions
1/2 cup coarsely chopped white onion
2 garlic cloves, minced
2 Scotch bonnet or habanero chiles, seeded and chopped
2 tablespoons each white vinegar and kosher salt
1 tablespoon each soy sauce and canola oil
2 teaspoons each chopped fresh thyme and fresh gingerroot
2 teaspoons packed brown sugar
1 teaspoon allspice
1/4 teaspoon each nutmeg and pepper
1/8 teaspoon cinnamon
1 (1 1/2-pound) pork tenderloin, trimmed

Combine all the ingredients except the tenderloin in a food processor. Process until smooth. Place the pork on a cutting board. Slice lengthwise to, but not through, the other side. Open the halves to lay flat. Slice each half lengthwise again to, but not through, the other side. Open to lay flat. Place the pork in a large resealable plastic bag. Add the onion mixture and seal the bag. Turn the bag several times to coat the pork with the onion mixture. Marinate in the refrigerator for 24 hours. Remove the pork from the bag and discard the marinade. Place the pork on a grill rack coated with nonstick cooking spray. Grill for 8 minutes per side or until 160 degrees on a meat thermometer and the pork is just slightly pink. Remove the pork to a cutting board and let stand for at least 5 minutes. Slice into bite-size pieces. Remove to a chafing dish and serve with wooden picks and forks.

Yield: 8 servings

*Note:* You can vary the degree of heat by using 1 less or up to 2 more chiles. We like the flavor with 2 chiles.

# Smoked Salmon Spread

10 ounces smoked salmon, coarsely chopped
2 cups sour cream
2 teaspoons capers, chopped
3 sweet gherkin pickles, chopped
1 tablespoon mayonnaise
1 tablespoon chopped fresh parsley
1/2 teaspoon minced garlic
1 to 2 pinches cayenne pepper, or to taste
1 baguette, thinly sliced and toasted

Combine the smoked salmon, sour cream, capers, pickles, mayonnaise, parsley, garlic and cayenne pepper in a bowl. Fold gently to mix. Cover and chill for 1 hour. Serve with the toasted baguette slices.

Yield: 8 servings

# Salmon Cups with Cucumber Sesame Salsa

1 cup finely chopped seeded peeled cucumber
1 jalapeño chile, seeded and finely chopped
2 teaspoons finely chopped fresh gingerroot
2 teaspoons sugar
1 teaspoon sesame oil
40 frozen miniature phyllo shells
1½ cups sour cream
1 pound smoked skinless salmon fillet, thinly sliced

Mix the cucumber, jalapeño chile, gingerroot, sugar and sesame oil in a bowl. Let stand for 1 hour. Arrange the frozen phyllo shells on a lightly greased baking sheet. Bake at 350 degrees for 7 minutes or until the edges are golden brown. Remove the shells to a wire rack to cool.

Spoon 1 teaspoon of the sour cream into each cooled phyllo cup. Top with a spoonful of the cucumber salsa. Top each with a rolled-up slice of salmon. Arrange the filled shells on a serving platter.

Yield: 8 to 10 servings

*Note:* Miniature phyllo shells are available in the freezer section of most grocery stores.

## Marinated Shrimp

1½ cups olive oil
½ cup chopped fresh parsley
4½ teaspoons dried basil
3 teaspoons dried oregano
12 garlic cloves, minced
2 tablespoons pepper
4½ teaspoons salt
¼ cup lemon juice
2 pounds deveined peeled shrimp
Lemon wedges for garnish

Mix the olive oil, parsley, basil, oregano, garlic, pepper, salt and lemon juice in a large bowl. Remove ⅓ of the mixture and set aside for basting. Add the shrimp to the remaining marinade. Stir to coat. Cover and chill for at least 1 hour. Soak wooden skewers in water for at least 1 hour.

Remove the shrimp from the marinade and thread onto the skewers. Discard the used marinade. Grill or broil the shrimp 3 minutes per side, basting often with the reserved marinade. Remove the skewers to a serving platter and garnish with lemon wedges.

Yield: 7 servings

*Note:* The aroma will get everyone's appetite going!

## Shrimp and Black Bean "Caviar"

4¹/2 cups water
1¹/2 pounds unpeeled medium shrimp
²/3 cup chunky salsa
1 (15-ounce) can black beans, drained
¹/2 cup chopped red onion
¹/4 cup finely chopped green bell pepper
¹/4 cup fresh lime juice
2 tablespoons chopped fresh cilantro
2 tablespoons canola oil
2 tablespoons honey
¹/4 teaspoon salt
Tortilla chips

Bring the water to a boil in a saucepan. Add the shrimp. Cook for 3 to 5 minutes or until the shrimp turn pink. Drain and rinse with cold water. Place the shrimp in a bowl, cover and chill. Peel, devein and finely chop the shrimp when cold. Combine the shrimp, salsa, black beans, onion, bell pepper, lime juice, cilantro, oil, honey and salt in a serving bowl. Stir to mix. Cover and chill for 2 to 4 hours, stirring occasionally. Serve with tortilla chips.

Yield: 14 servings

## Citrus-Marinated Shrimp Cocktail

1 cup orange juice
1 cup fresh lemon juice
3/4 cup ketchup
1/3 cup vodka
1/4 teaspoon hot sauce
1/4 cup olive oil
1 1/2 pounds peeled cooked large shrimp
1 small red onion, very thinly sliced (about 1 3/4 cups)
1 cup finely chopped fresh cilantro

Whisk the orange juice, lemon juice, ketchup, vodka and hot
sauce in a large bowl. Whisk in the olive oil. Add the shrimp, onion
and cilantro. Stir to mix well. Cover and chill for at least 3 hours
and up to 6 hours. Remove the shrimp from the marinade to
a serving platter.

Yield: 6 to 8 servings

## Hap's Famous Rémoulade Sauce

1 cup canola oil
1/2 cup vinegar
1/4 cup horseradish mustard
2 tablespoons ketchup
1 tablespoon paprika
1 teaspoon salt
1/2 teaspoon cayenne pepper
1/2 cup chopped green onions
1/2 cup chopped celery
1 garlic clove, chopped

Combine the oil, vinegar, horseradish mustard, ketchup, paprika, salt, cayenne pepper, green onions, celery and garlic in a food processor or blender. Process until thoroughly blended and smooth.

Yield: 2 cups

*Note:* This flavorful sauce is excellent to serve alongside some boiled or steamed shrimp. It will keep in the refrigerator for 1 week. If you can't use it all with shrimp, try it with grilled chicken or as a salad dressing.

# Curry Chicken Spread

2 cups (8 ounces) shredded Monterey Jack cheese
6 ounces cream cheese, softened
1/4 cup chopped green onions
2/3 cup Major Grey's chutney
1 tablespoon curry powder
1 teaspoon ginger
1/2 teaspoon salt
3 boneless skinless chicken breast halves,
cooked and shredded
1 cup sour cream
1/2 teaspoon garlic powder
1/4 teaspoon paprika
1/4 teaspoon pepper
3/4 cup chopped green onions
1/4 to 1/2 cup raisins
1/2 cup slivered or sliced almonds, toasted
Wheat crackers

Beat the Monterey Jack cheese, cream cheese, 1/4 cup green onions, chutney, curry powder, ginger and salt in a bowl until well mixed. Spread thinly onto a large serving platter. Cover and chill. Mix the chicken, sour cream, garlic powder, paprika and pepper in a bowl. Spread over the cheese layer on the platter. Cover and chill for 4 to 24 hours. Sprinkle 3/4 cup green onions around the edge of the cheese mixture when ready to serve. Sprinkle the raisins and almonds over the center. Serve with wheat crackers.

Yield: 18 servings

*Note:* Your party guests will rave about this one!

## Bacon and Tomato Spread

8 ounces cream cheese, softened
2 teaspoons prepared yellow mustard
1/2 teaspoon celery salt
6 slices bacon, crisp-cooked and crumbled
1 tomato, peeled, seeded and finely chopped
1/4 cup finely chopped green bell pepper
Melba rounds, crackers or toast points

Beat the cream cheese, mustard and celery salt in a bowl. Stir in the bacon, chopped tomato and bell pepper. Cover and chill. Serve in a small bowl and surround with melba rounds, crackers or toast points.

Yield: 6 to 8 servings

## Stilton Cheese Spread with Pears

12 ounces cream cheese, cut into cubes and softened
1/2 cup (1 stick) butter, cut into cubes and softened
8 ounces Stilton cheese, crumbled and softened
1/2 cup chopped walnuts, toasted
2 pears, peeled, cored and sliced
Crackers

Combine the cream cheese and butter in a food processor. Pulse until blended. Add the Stilton cheese and pulse until mixed. Press the cheese mixture evenly into a 7-inch springform pan lined with plastic wrap. Cover and chill for 3 hours or until firm. Remove the side of the pan and invert the cheese mixture onto a plate. Remove the bottom of the pan and the plastic wrap. Invert the cheese mixture onto a serving platter. Let stand at room temperature for 1 hour. Smooth any cracks with a wet knife. Sprinkle the cheese with the walnuts and surround with pear slices and crackers.

Yield: 10 servings

*Note:* Wait until just before serving to slice the pears
so they won't brown.

## Stone Hill Cheese Spread

8 ounces cream cheese, softened
1 garlic clove, minced
1 tablespoon grated onion
3½ tablespoons butter
¼ cup packed dark brown sugar
1 teaspoon Worcestershire sauce
½ teaspoon prepared yellow mustard
1 cup finely chopped pecans
Assorted mild crackers
Fresh fruit

Combine the cream cheese, garlic and onion in a bowl. Stir with a fork until well mixed. Spread the mixture into a 1×6-inch disk on a serving plate, using a spatula. Cover and chill. Melt the butter in a saucepan. Add the brown sugar, Worcestershire sauce and mustard and stir well. Add the pecans and stir well to mix. Cook for 3 to 4 minutes to release the oils in the pecans, stirring often. Remove from the heat and let cool for 2 to 3 minutes. Top the chilled cheese spread with the nut mixture so that no cheese shows. Chill until 1 hour before ready to serve. Serve at room temperature with crackers and fresh fruit.

Yield: 6 servings

*Note:* This recipe always has people guessing as to the ingredients. It's a wonderful combination, with the outside layer ending up tasting almost like a praline. We have never shared this recipe until now.

# Eggplant Spread

1/3 cup olive oil
3 cups chopped peeled eggplant
1 onion, chopped
1 cup sliced fresh mushrooms
1/3 cup chopped green bell pepper
2 or 3 garlic cloves, minced
1 (6-ounce) can tomato paste
1 (5³/4-ounce) jar pitted green olives, drained and chopped
2 tablespoons red wine vinegar
1¹/2 teaspoons sugar
1 teaspoon salt
1/2 teaspoon coarsely ground pepper
1/4 teaspoon hot sauce
1 loaf French bread, sliced

Heat the olive oil in a large skillet over medium heat. Add the eggplant, onion, mushrooms, bell pepper and garlic and sauté for 10 minutes or until the vegetables are tender. Stir in the tomato paste, olives, vinegar, sugar, salt, pepper and hot sauce. Bring to a boil and reduce the heat. Simmer for 30 to 40 minutes or to desired thickness, stirring occasionally. Serve warm or at room temperature with slices of French bread.

Yield: 4 cups

*Note:* Amazingly, people who say they usually don't care for eggplant often love this spread. This will keep in the refrigerator for up to 1 week.

## White Bean Spread and Garlic Crostini

2 (15-ounce) cans cannellini beans, rinsed and well drained
4 sun-dried tomato halves packed in oil, drained and chopped
2 tablespoons chopped fresh basil or parsley
2 tablespoons olive oil
2 tablespoons lemon juice
2 garlic cloves, minced
1/4 teaspoon salt
1/8 teaspoon pepper
1 baguette, cut into 1/4- to 3/8-inch-thick slices
1/4 cup olive oil
2 garlic cloves, halved

Combine the beans, sun-dried tomatoes, basil, 2 tablespoons olive oil, lemon juice, minced garlic, salt and pepper in a food processor. Pulse until the beans are mashed but retain some texture. Remove the mixture to a serving dish. Cover and chill until 30 minutes before ready to serve.

Arrange the bread slices on a baking sheet covered with parchment paper. Brush with 1/4 cup olive oil. Bake at 400 degrees for 5 to 7 minutes or until lightly toasted. Remove the toasted slices to a wire rack and let cool slightly. Rub the toasted sides with the cut sides of the garlic clove halves. Serve the crostini along with the spread. A bowl of olives makes a nice accompaniment.

Yield: 8 to 10 servings

*Note:* If you don't have parchment paper, just use
an ungreased baking sheet.

## Artichoke Dip

2 cups mayonnaise
2 cups (8 ounces) grated Parmesan cheese
4 garlic cloves, minced
1 tablespoon garlic salt
1 tablespoon Worcestershire sauce
1 tablespoon lemon juice
2 teaspoons black pepper
1 teaspoon paprika
$1/2$ to 1 teaspoon cayenne pepper, or to taste
2 dashes Tabasco sauce
6 (14-ounce) cans artichoke hearts, squeezed dry and
chopped into large pieces
Grated Parmesan cheese
Baguette slices or crackers

Mix the mayonnaise, 2 cups Parmesan cheese, garlic, garlic salt,
Worcestershire sauce, lemon juice, black pepper, paprika, cayenne
pepper and Tabasco sauce in a large bowl. Add the artichoke hearts
and stir to mix well. Spoon into a chafing dish and sprinkle with
additional Parmesan cheese. Bake at 350 degrees for 45 to 50 minutes
or until light brown. Serve with baguette slices or crackers.

Yield: 16 servings

*Note:* We serve this in a chafing dish. If you don't have one, just
use an ovenproof dish and serve immediately.

# Layered Mediterranean Dip

2 (15-ounce) cans black beans, rinsed, drained and mashed
1/2 cup chopped tomato
1/2 cup chopped cucumber
1/3 cup sliced black olives
1/4 cup chopped green onions
1 tablespoon olive oil
1 teaspoon Greek seasoning
4 ounces tomato-basil feta cheese, crumbled
Pita chips

Spread the mashed beans in a shallow 9-inch dish. Combine the tomato, cucumber, olives, green onions, olive oil and Greek seasoning in a bowl. Toss to mix. Sprinkle over the mashed bean layer. Top with the cheese. Cover and chill thoroughly. Serve with pita chips.

Yield: 10 to 12 servings

## Texas "Caviar"

1 (15-ounce) can yellow hominy, drained
1 (15-ounce) can black-eyed peas, drained
3 green onions, finely chopped
2 garlic cloves, minced
1 large tomato, chopped
1 green bell pepper, chopped
1 jalapeño chile, seeded and finely chopped
1/3 cup chopped fresh parsley
1/4 cup chopped yellow onion
1/2 cup Zesty Italian salad dressing
Tortilla chips

Mix the hominy, black-eyed peas, green onions, garlic, tomato, bell pepper, jalapeño chile, parsley and yellow onion in a bowl. Add the salad dressing and toss gently to mix. Cover and chill thoroughly. Toss again just before serving with tortilla chips.

Yield: 10 servings

## Black Bean and Corn Salsa

3 ears of fresh white corn
3/4 cup water
3 tomatoes, peeled, seeded and finely chopped
2 jalapeño chiles, seeded and finely chopped
2 (15-ounce) cans black beans, rinsed and drained
1 cup chopped fresh cilantro
1/3 cup fresh lime juice
1/4 teaspoon salt
1/4 teaspoon pepper
2 avocados
Tortilla chips

Cut the corn from the cobs and place in a saucepan. Add the water and bring to a boil. Cover and reduce the heat. Cook for 6 to 7 minutes or until the corn is tender; drain. Combine the corn, tomatoes, jalapeño chiles, black beans, cilantro, lime juice, salt and pepper in a bowl. Stir gently to mix. Cover and chill. Peel, pit and finely chop the avocados just before serving time. Add to the corn mixture and stir gently to mix. Serve with tortilla chips.

Yield: 14 servings

## Bruschetta with Summer Vegetables

1 small red onion, chopped
1/2 cucumber, peeled and chopped
2 large tomatoes, peeled, seeded and chopped
1 1/4 teaspoons sea salt
1/8 teaspoon oregano
1/4 cup chopped fresh flat-leaf parsley
1/4 cup finely chopped fresh basil
1/8 teaspoon (or less) crushed red pepper
4 1/2 teaspoons olive oil
Salt and pepper to taste
8 (1/2-inch-thick) slices rustic or Italian bread

Mix the onion, cucumber and tomatoes in a bowl. Sprinkle with the sea salt. Let stand at room temperature for 2 hours.

Drain the liquid from the vegetables. Stir in the oregano, parsley, basil and crushed red pepper. Add the olive oil and toss to mix. Season with salt and pepper.

Arrange the bread slices on a baking sheet. Place under a preheated broiler for about 30 seconds. Turn the bread and broil the other side for 30 to 60 seconds or until lightly toasted. Remove the bread to a serving platter or plates. Top with the vegetable mixture and let stand at room temperature for 1 hour before serving.

Yield: 4 servings

*Note:* To easily peel ripe tomatoes, dip them in boiling water for 1 minute or until the skins split. Remove with a slotted spoon and slip off the skins.

## Asiago Cheese Cups

1/4 cup sun-dried tomatoes, coarsely chopped
1/2 cup water
12 ounces cream cheese, softened
1 cup (4 ounces) grated asiago cheese
1/4 cup mayonnaise
2 tablespoons grated Parmesan cheese
2 tablespoons fresh basil, chopped
30 frozen miniature phyllo shells

Combine the sun-dried tomatoes and water in a small bowl. Let stand for 2 hours or until rehydrated; drain. Combine the cream cheese, asiago cheese, mayonnaise and Parmesan cheese in a bowl. Beat with an electric mixer at medium speed until blended. Stir in the sun-dried tomatoes and basil. Spoon the mixture into a pastry bag fitted with a large tip. Arrange the frozen phyllo shells on a lightly greased baking sheet. Pipe the cheese mixture into the phyllo shells. Bake at 350 degrees for 10 minutes or until the edges of the shells are beginning to brown. Remove to a serving platter and serve warm.

Yield: 6 servings

*Note:* Miniature phyllo shells are available in the freezer section of most grocery stores.

## Savory Mushroom Cups

2 tablespoons butter, softened
1 (1-pound) loaf thinly sliced firm white bread
1/4 cup (1/2 stick) butter
3 shallots, minced
8 ounces fresh mushrooms, finely chopped
2 tablespoons flour
1/2 cup heavy cream
3 tablespoons fresh or freeze-dried chives
2 tablespoons chopped fresh parsley
1/2 teaspoon lemon juice
1/2 teaspoon salt
1/8 teaspoon cayenne pepper
2 tablespoons grated Parmesan cheese

Grease the insides of 24 miniature muffin cups with 2 tablespoons butter. Cut a 2 1/2- to 3-inch round from each slice of bread using a plain or fluted cutter. Press the bread rounds into the buttered miniature muffin cups to line the bottom and sides. Bake at 400 degrees for 10 minutes or until golden brown. Remove the toast cups to a wire rack to cool completely.

Melt ¼ cup butter in a large skillet over medium heat. Add the shallots and sauté for 2 minutes or until tender but not brown. Add the mushrooms and sauté for 10 to 15 minutes or until most of the liquid evaporates. Sprinkle the flour over the mushrooms and cook for 2 minutes, stirring constantly. Increase the heat to high and stir in the heavy cream. Cook for 3 minutes or until the mixture comes to a boil, stirring constantly. Remove from the heat and stir in the chives, parsley, lemon juice, salt and cayenne pepper.

Arrange the toast cups on a lightly greased baking sheet. Spoon about 1 tablespoon of the mushroom mixture into each toast cup and sprinkle each with ¼ teaspoon grated Parmesan cheese. Bake at 350 degrees for 10 minutes or until the tops are golden brown and the filling is bubbly.

Yield: 8 servings

*Note:* The toast cups can be stored in an airtight container for up to 3 days or frozen. The mushroom filling can be stored, tightly covered, in the refrigerator for up to 3 days.

# Sun-Dried Tomato Topped Goat Cheese

10 sun-dried tomato halves
3 garlic cloves, minced
2 tablespoons olive oil
1 tablespoon chopped fresh rosemary
1 baguette, thinly sliced
Olive oil for brushing
1 (11-ounce) log, or 3 (3-ounce) logs, goat cheese
Fresh rosemary sprigs for garnish

Cover the sun-dried tomatoes with boiling water in a small bowl; let stand for 5 minutes. Drain and chop. Mix the sun-dried tomatoes, garlic, 2 tablespoons olive oil and chopped rosemary in a bowl. Cover and chill for up to 4 hours.

Arrange the bread slices on an ungreased baking sheet. Brush with olive oil. Bake at 350 degrees for 8 minutes or until lightly toasted. Remove the slices to a wire rack to cool.

Place the goat cheese on a serving plate. Top with the sun-dried tomato mixture and garnish with sprigs of rosemary. Serve with the toasted baguette slices.

Yield: 8 servings

## Savory Layered Torta

1 cup (2 sticks) chilled butter, cut into pieces
12 ounces feta cheese, crumbled
8 ounces cream cheese, softened
2 garlic cloves, chopped
1 shallot, chopped
1/2 cup white wine
1/2 cup pine nuts, lightly toasted
1 cup sun-dried tomatoes packed in oil,
drained and finely chopped
1 cup prepared pesto
French bread slices or crackers

Combine the butter, feta cheese, cream cheese, garlic, shallot
and wine in a food processor or blender. Process until smooth.
Lightly oil a 4×8-inch loaf pan. Line with plastic wrap, allowing
extra plastic wrap to hang over the sides. Sprinkle half the pine nuts
in the bottom of the pan. Top with half the sun-dried tomatoes
and then spread with half the pesto. Spread half the cheese mixture
over the pesto layer. Repeat the layers with the remaining pine nuts,
sun-dried tomatoes, pesto and cheese mixture. Fold the plastic
wrap over the top, pressing to smooth. Chill for at least 1 hour or
overnight until firm.

Unwrap and invert onto a serving platter. Remove the plastic wrap.
Serve with French bread slices or crackers.

Yield: 18 servings

# Savory Artichoke Cheesecake

### CRUST
2 tablespoons butter, softened
1/4 cup bread crumbs
1/4 cup (1 ounce) grated Parmesan cheese
1 1/2 teaspoons finely chopped fresh basil
1 1/2 teaspoons finely chopped fresh tarragon

### FILLING
16 ounces cream cheese, softened
1 cup (4 ounces) crumbled feta cheese
1 cup sour cream
3 eggs
1 (14-ounce) can artichoke hearts, drained and chopped
1 small green bell pepper, chopped
2 tablespoons chopped red bell pepper
6 green onions, chopped
1 large garlic clove, minced
1 tablespoon chopped fresh basil
1 tablespoon chopped fresh tarragon
1 teaspoon salt
1/2 teaspoon pepper
Fresh basil sprigs for garnish
Mild crackers

*For the crust,* grease a 9- or 10-inch springform pan with the butter. Mix the bread crumbs, Parmesan cheese, basil and tarragon in a small bowl. Add to the springform pan and tilt to coat with the crumb mixture. Tap out any excess.

*For the filling,* beat the cream cheese in a large bowl with an electric mixer until light and fluffy. Add the feta cheese and sour cream. Beat until well mixed, scraping down the side of the bowl often while beating. Add the eggs. Beat until well mixed, scraping down the side of the bowl often while beating. Add the artichoke hearts, green bell pepper, red bell pepper, green onions, garlic, basil, tarragon, salt and pepper. Beat to mix well. Spoon into the pan. Bake at 350 degrees for 55 minutes or until golden brown. Remove to a wire rack and let cool to room temperature. Cover and chill in the pan for at least 2 hours. Loosen from the side of the pan with a sharp knife and remove the side. Set the cheesecake on a cake plate and garnish with sprigs of basil. Serve with crackers.

Yield: 16 to 20 servings

*Note:* This recipe is a variation of one we originally got from The Inn at the Round Barn Farm in Waitsfield, Vermont.

## *Mexican Cheesecake*

1¹/₂ cups finely crushed tortilla chips
¹/₄ cup (¹/₂ stick) butter, melted
16 ounces cream cheese, softened
2 cups (8 ounces) shredded Monterey Jack cheese
1 cup sour cream
3 eggs
1 cup mild salsa
1 (4-ounce) can chopped green chiles
1 cup sour cream
3 avocados
1 tomato, seeded and chopped
1 tablespoon lemon juice
1 teaspoon salt
1 teaspoon (or more) cumin
1 cup mild salsa, drained
Tortilla chips

Combine the crushed tortilla chips and melted butter in a bowl. Stir to mix well. Press in the bottom of a lightly greased 9-inch springform pan. Bake at 350 degrees for 10 minutes. Remove to a wire rack.

134

Combine the cream cheese and Monterey Jack cheese in a large bowl. Beat with an electric mixer until light and fluffy. Beat in 1 cup sour cream. Add the eggs and beat at low speed until the ingredients are just combined. Stir in 1 cup salsa and the green chiles. Pour over the tortilla crust in the pan. Bake at 350 degrees for 50 to 60 minutes or until the center is almost set. Remove to a wire rack. Spread 1 cup sour cream over the top. Let cool to room temperature. Cover and chill for at least 3 hours and up to 24 hours.

Peel, pit and mash the avocados in a bowl 1 hour before serving time. Add the tomato, lemon juice, salt and cumin. Stir with a fork until combined. Cover and chill.

Loosen the cheesecake from the side of the pan with a sharp knife and remove the side. Set the cheesecake on a serving platter. Dollop the avocado mixture alternately with 1 cup drained salsa around the edge of the cheesecake. Serve with tortilla chips.

Yield: 20 servings

*Note:* This festive savory cheesecake will feed a hungry crowd. It's a recipe that has been requested dozens of times, and we have not shared it until now.

# Pizza Rustica

## DOUGH
2 cups plus 2 tablespoons flour
1/2 teaspoon sea salt
7 tablespoons chilled unsalted butter, cut into pieces
2 eggs, at room temperature
2 tablespoons cold water (if needed)

## FILLING
6 ounces mozzarella cheese, cut into cubes
5 ounces thick-sliced ham, cut into cubes
5 ounces thick-sliced salami, cut into cubes
5 ounces young sheep's milk cheese, such as pecorino dolce,
pecorino sardo, caciotta or Greek sheep's milk cheese
5 ounces ricotta cheese, drained
3 eggs
3 tablespoons freshly grated Parmigiano-Reggiano cheese
Salt and pepper to taste
1 egg white, beaten

*For the dough,* combine the flour and sea salt in a bowl. Cut in the butter with a pastry blender until it resembles coarse cornmeal. Add the eggs 1 at a time, beating well after each addition. Add the water if the dough is too dry. Knead the dough on a lightly floured surface for 2 minutes or until smooth. Wrap the dough in plastic wrap and chill for 1 hour.

*For the filling,* mix the mozzarella cheese, ham, salami and sheep's milk cheese in a large bowl. Stir the ricotta cheese in a bowl. Add the eggs 1 at a time, beating well after each addition. Pour into the meat mixture and stir to mix. Stir in the Parmigiano-Reggiano cheese and season with salt and pepper.

Divide the dough into 2 pieces, one being twice the size of the other. Roll out the large piece on a lightly floured surface to a 13-inch circle. Fit the circle into a well-oiled 9-inch springform pan, making sure the dough hangs over the edge. Spread the filling over the dough in the pan. Roll out the remaining piece of dough on a lightly floured surface to a 9½-inch circle. Place on top of the filling. Pinch the edges of the 2 layers of dough together to seal. Prick the top crust with a fork and brush with the beaten egg white. Bake at 400 degrees for 45 to 50 minutes or until the top is golden brown. Remove to a wire rack and let cool. Loosen the pizza from the side of the pan with a sharp knife and remove the side. Set the pizza on a serving platter and cut into wedges. Serve at room temperature.

Yield: 10 servings

*Note:* This also makes a wonderful supper with a green salad.

## Antipasto Bowl

3 cups fresh asparagus tips
3 cups quartered button mushrooms
1 cup red bell pepper strips
1/2 cup pitted black olives
3 ounces part-skim mozzarella cheese, cut into cubes
1 (14-ounce) can artichoke hearts, drained and quartered
1 (11 1/2-ounce) jar pickled pepperoncini peppers, drained
1/3 cup cider vinegar
1/4 cup finely chopped fresh parsley
3 garlic cloves, minced
2 tablespoons olive oil
2 teaspoons dried oregano
1 teaspoon sugar
1/4 teaspoon salt
1/4 teaspoon pepper

Cook the asparagus tips in a covered steamer for 2 minutes or until just blanched. Plunge into ice water; drain well. Combine the asparagus, mushrooms, bell pepper strips, olives, cheese, artichoke hearts and pepperoncini peppers in a large bowl. Whisk the vinegar, parsley, garlic, olive oil, oregano, sugar, salt and pepper in a bowl. Pour over the vegetable mixture and toss gently to coat. Cover and chill for 2 hours, stirring occasionally. Serve chilled or at room temperature with forks.

Yield: 16 servings

*Note:* This is a great appetizer to serve when you know you'll be entertaining people on low-carb diets.

# Index

Stone Hill Inn, Inc.
89 Houston Farm Road
Stowe, Vermont 05672-4225
802-253-6282
stay@stonehillinn.com

Name
_____

Street Address
_____

City                                    State          Zip
_____

Telephone

| YOUR ORDER | QTY | TOTAL |
|---|---|---|
| *The Signature Recipe Collection* at $22.95 each | | $ |
| Vermont residents add 6% sales tax | | $ |
| Postage & handling at $3.50 US Postal Service book rate; $6.00 US Postal Service Priority Mail | | $ |
| | TOTAL | $ |

Method of Payment:   [   ]  American Express   [   ]  Diners Club
                                 [   ]  Discover   [   ]  MasterCard   [   ]  VISA
                                 [   ]  Check payable to Stone Hill Inn, Inc.

Account Number                                    Expiration Date
_____

Signature

*Photocopies accepted.*